THE
ABC'S
OF
BALLROOM DANCE

Second Edition

Suzanne Marie Zelnik-Geldys

Eastern Michigan University

KENDALL/HUNT PUBLISHING COMPANY
4050 Westmark Drive Dubuque, Iowa 52002

To all students of ballroom dance

CONTENTS

PREFACE

Ballroom dance is a lifetime activity, one enjoyed round the world by young and old alike. Dance is so integral to human life that almost every culture has had some form of physical expression that can be defined as dance. Dance is an age old expression of joy and happiness, "song and dance the crown of a feast." (Homer) Moreover, dance has a rejuvenating, uplifting quality; it evokes man's most primal emotions. "The dance—it is the rhythm of all that dies in order to live again; it is the eternal rising of the sun." (Art 101 Limited dance poster)

I became interested in ballroom dance during one of the most difficult periods of my life and found it to be almost therapeutic. Even today, many years later, no matter how rotten my mood, within 20 minutes of dancing, I feel better. I used to think that if you could walk, you could dance but when disco was popular my husband and I frequented a disco club located across the street from a Veteran's Administration hospital. In that club we were introduced to some extraordinary wheelchair dancing with gravity defying one wheel spins and I quickly discovered that you don't need to walk to dance. Dance is truly such a natural means of self-expression that it transcends handicaps, crosses generations and is enjoyed by all nationalities throughout the world.

Ballroom dance is a healthy form of exercise which relieves stress. It is a social activity providing an opportunity to meet others and to form friendships. It is a lifetime activity and is truly intergenerational. People of all ages—children, teenagers, parents and grandparents—can all enjoy ballroom dancing and sometimes even get a chance to dance with one another at weddings or other events. Dance also affords an opportunity for creative expression.

This book is designed to be used as an instructional tool for beginning and continuing ballroom dancers whether they're enrolled in a college, university or community education ballroom class or even if they're learning on their own. It can be kept as a resource book and be used to revive the dancer's memory of patterns and to review dance foundations and technique, something which even professional dancers need to do.

Ballroom dance is far more than "steps." A good leader must be able to lead his partner and his partner must be able to follow whatever is led. The purpose of this book is to teach proper leading using body leads and proper following so that students can dance with anyone anywhere no matter what steps are used. Since the basis of good leading and following is the dance frame, special emphasis will be placed on using and maintaining the proper frame in each dance.

The book is divided into three sections. Part I is devoted to the foundations of ballroom dance, those aspects of dance which students need to begin dancing and those which need to be reviewed often by all dancers. Part II deals with smooth dance technique, fox trot, waltz and tango. Part III covers rhythm dance technique, rumba, cha-cha, mambo, samba, swing and polka.

Each dance chapter begins with a brief history of the dance and then discusses the rhythm, rhythm time signature, proper dance frame and correct technique. Common patterns in each dance are then presented using a format which is easy to read and to follow. Each pattern is described in step by step detail with specific directions including which foot is used, the direction the foot moves, the degree and direction of turn, the musical count, the lead and any special technique. Although the leader's and follower's parts are presented separately, followers should read the leader's part, paying close attention to the *Note* for this is where the lead is described.

The dance proverbs are an easy and sometimes humorous way to remember some of the basic principles of ballroom dance. The glossary is designed to clarify ballroom dance terminology. The bibliography is annotated for those who wish to continue their reading in ballroom dance and the index makes this book a handy reference tool.

ACKNOWLEDGMENTS

My thanks: First to my family—Jerry, Laura and Lisa—for their patience and support.

To my parents, Bob and Nelly, for helping as proofreaders.

To the friends whose efforts as proofreaders, photographers and helpers made this project possible: Patricia Cherney, Nonni Counter, Tom DesJardins, Carol DiSabatino, Vern Fath, Jan Haag and Shelly Clipson.

To the friends and fellow dancers who were models for the photographs: Max Ali, Nonni Counter, Tom DesJardins, Vern Fath, Kathy Kowalske and Ken Robinson.

To all my wonderful dance instructors, especially Sheri Mygal and her partner, Dave Maurice.

To Nancy Ireland whose help as typist and proofreader was invaluable.

In memory of: Jury Gotshalks who helped me unlock what I hold inside, the whole person that I am, and who helped me express this in my dance.

GETTING STARTED

Posture

Dance posture refers to standing and moving with the body in proper alignment. Good dance posture begins with good daily posture.

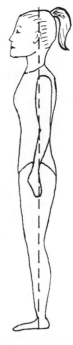

Ideal daily posture

But since dance is presentational, a good dancer must look slightly larger than life. He must *come to dance:* grow an extra 1/2 inch, creating space between the ribs like an accordion which is expanded, and keep his head up with eyes looking out. The shoulders should be relaxed, neither pushed up like a football player nor rotated back like a soldier. In all dances the body weight should be placed over the balls of the feet and the arms kept in front of the body.

Dance Frames

> . . . *Dance is the only art of which we ourselves are the stuff of which it is made.* (Ted Shawn)

Dance is living moving sculpture and the starting point of this sculpture is the dance frame. Couples with good dance frames are not only attractive on the dance floor but also successful at leading and following.

The Good   The Bad   The Ugly

For **closed dance position** the partners stand slightly off-center with toes and hips facing each other. The man places his right wrist bone under her left armpit so that each can feel the other; he rotates his right biceps down and points his right fingers down in a straight line to help keep his elbows from dropping. He extends his left arm, bending it at the elbow with left palm facing toward his partner and placed in between the two of them. His fingers curl over hers. The partners exert equal resistance, his left hand to her right; they are like walls for each other neither pushing nor pulling, but solidly there. Following the *rule of thumb,* he places his thumb at eye level if the partners are the same height or divides the difference in their eye levels if the partners are different heights. The man and woman should be thumb to thumb; if she hooks him it is easier for her to take over the lead dragging him where he may not want to go. (p. 9.) Each partner should form a long level line extending from one elbow across the back to the other elbow so that someone could stretch a tape measure across the dancer's back. Each partner should have both of his sides equally stretched and each should stay slightly to the left of the other's centerline. The woman gently wraps the thumb and fingers of her L hand around his R biceps resting her L forearm on his arm. (p. 9.) The couple should appear symmetrical. Each partner should look at eye level over the other partner's right shoulder. Once they are in dance position there should be a small breathing space between them. The woman's body should form a diagonal line from the top of her head to the bottom of her right toe; she should feel his wrist bone under her arm.

Closed dance position

Lady's position

Stay left

In **promenade or conversation position** the man's top line is extended to his greatest spread, that is the distance from one elbow to the other is fully stretched without changing his hand or arm position. Even though his step is to his left his shoulders rotate ever so *slightly* to the right. Both partners apply the *nose follows toes rule* so that their heads look down line of dance. In the second step of promenade the man steps into **contrary body movement position.** This position is reached whenever either foot is placed across the front or the back of the body without the body turning.

Man's top line in promenade

Partners looking in promenade

Contrary body movement position in the second step of promenade

Right outside partner and **left outside partner** can each be used in closed or open position. These are sometimes called right and left parallel positions. The key here is to keep one half of the partner's body covered. Sometimes when the dancer steps outside his partner, he will be using contrary body movement position.

Right outside partner;
closed dance position

Left outside partner; open
position

The **Latin closed dance frame** is slightly more rounded than the smooth. Partners practice getting into this position by standing in front of one another and raising their arms up and down like railroad crossing gates. Then the partners press his L forearm to her R forearm giving one another equal resistance. Her L hand is placed in the hollow at the front of his R shoulder. The space between the partners' upper bodies is more oval than it is in smooth dance.

Railroad gates   Latin closed position

Swing has two major dance frames: in the **open position** the couple is face to face and hand to hand. The hands should be held in a "neutral zone," an imaginary line that falls in between the couple; they should be held between the waist and the hips, at the center of the partners' bodies. Once again, the partners will exert equal resistance. Their point of connection will be in their hands. In **closed position** an open hand hold is used with the left hand (p. 11) while a more traditional closed dance position is maintained with the rest of the body. In either position the arms are held fairly close to the body, but with a slight breathing space.

Swing open position   Swing closed position

In the **sweetheart** or **varsouvienne position** the dancers are side by side. This position is R hand to R hand and L hand to L hand. The hands may be held high or low. This position is used in polka, Jesse polka, some of the Latin dances and hustle.

Sweetheart position

Foot Positions

The foot positions used in ballroom dance are shared with all forms of dance and are borrowed from ballet. The degree of turn out, or rotation of the toes, will vary from dance to dance and pattern to pattern.

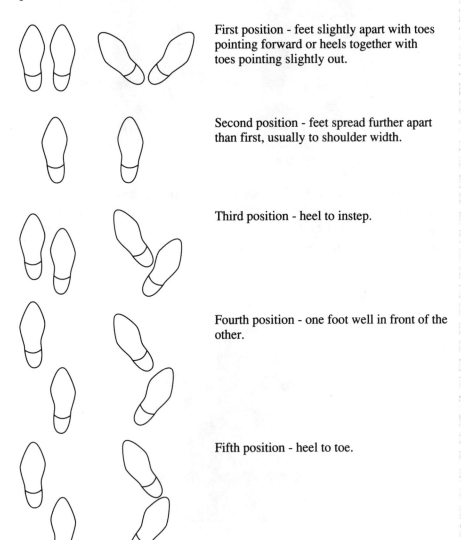

First position - feet slightly apart with toes pointing forward or heels together with toes pointing slightly out.

Second position - feet spread further apart than first, usually to shoulder width.

Third position - heel to instep.

Fourth position - one foot well in front of the other.

Fifth position - heel to toe.

Hand Holds

The hand holds will vary from dance to dance and pattern to pattern.

Smooth dance: thumb to thumb

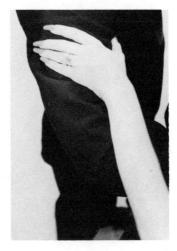

Smooth dance: woman's hand wrapped around man's biceps

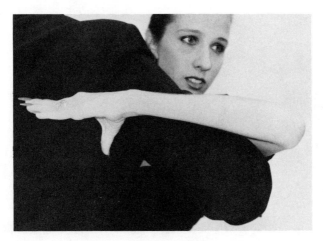

Tango: woman's thumb underneath man's underarm or triceps; fingers extended to form a straight line

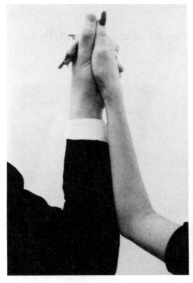

Latin dance: forearm to forearm

Latin dance: woman's hand pressed into man's shoulder

To change from the regular Latin hand hold to the pistol, the man slides his thumb to the side of her first finger, then turns his thumb on top of her knuckles and ends in a hook.

Latin dance: pistol hand hold—start

Latin dance: pistol hand hold—middle

Latin dance: pistol hand hold—end

Swing: woman's hooks to man's thumbs across the top

Double hand hold: fingers around partner's hand

Arm Styling

Styling is to dance what spices are to cooking. The styling of the dancers can create excitement and be highly creative and unique. Styling that is appropriate in one dance may be totally unsuitable in another and styling that looks terrific on one person may be horrible on another. Only very basic arm styling, if any, is mentioned in the breakdown of patterns. More exciting styling can be substituted. A few ideas are shown in the pictures that follow. Students with a good eye for line are encouraged to be inventive and creative. No matter what styling is used, students must remember not to hyper-extend the elbow or shoulder joints and not to break the line at the wrist.

Arm travels in towards the body

Arm travels out to the
side—all dances

Hand on hip—rhythm dances

Arm swings—rhythm dances

Arm up—rhythm dances

Arm down—rhythm
dances

Arm crossed across
body—all dances

Jazz hand—rhythm dances

Pointed finger-swing   Hand to upper belly—Latin

Arm through the hair—rhythm   Arm around partner's neck—all dances
dances

The arms should always be held in front of the body. Basic arm styling can be practiced against a wall. The dancer faces the wall extending his arms down in front of his body so the knuckles touch the wall. Maintaining the wall contact, he raises the arms to the chest so that the fingertips almost touch and then extends them out to the sides and back down again. Thumbs should be on the top as the arms are raised and on the bottom as the arms are lowered. The purpose is to train the dancer to keep the arms in front of his body and to learn to flex the elbows and let the elbow lead the lower arm.

Line of Dance

All traffic on the dance floor moves like runners around the race track in a counterclockwise direction. This direction of travel is referred to as line of dance.

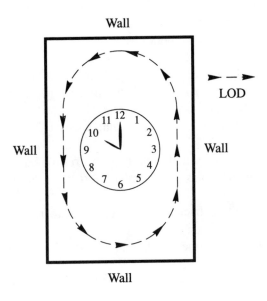

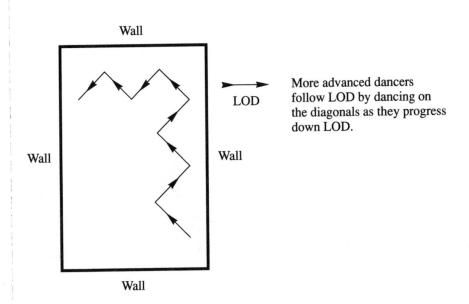

More advanced dancers follow LOD by dancing on the diagonals as they progress down LOD.

Direction of Movement

In ballroom dance the feet and the body have a specially defined relationship to the room that enables dancers to describe the flow of the movement within patterns. Some people call this alignment but since the term alignment is also widely used to describe proper dance posture, direction of movement seems less confusing. Six terms are used to define direction of movement:

1. *Wall* refers to any of the four walls in the room.
2. *Facing* refers to the body and feet placed face front.
3. *Backing* refers to the body and feet placed with the back leading; in closed dance position, if the man faces LOD the lady will be backing LOD.
4. *Center* is not the actual center of the room; but rather, the part of the room which is on the man's left when he is facing line of dance.
5. *Against* refers to backward movement that opposes the line of dance.
6. *Diagonal* refers to the points that are 45° from line of dance.

Wall

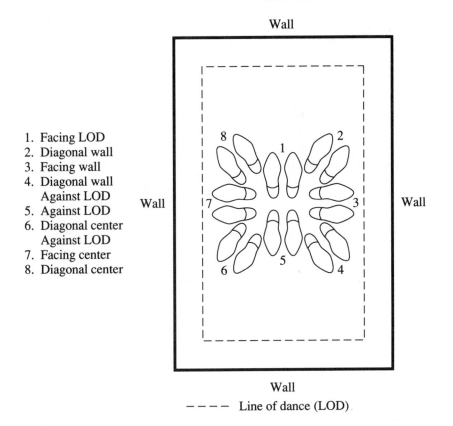

1. Facing LOD
2. Diagonal wall
3. Facing wall
4. Diagonal wall
   Against LOD
5. Against LOD
6. Diagonal center
   Against LOD
7. Facing center
8. Diagonal center

Wall

Wall

Wall

– – – – Line of dance (LOD)

Leading and Following

In the words of the song, "Love and marriage go together like a horse and carriage—you can't have one without the other." (Sammy Cahn) So, too, are leading and following an inseparable duo. The best female dancer can dance only what her partner leads and the best male can go only where his partner can follow. The key to success at leading and following is a good dance frame! Since all of the leads come from the man's body, the woman must be able to feel where her partner is going.

The man's responsibilities:

1. Because the man selects the step patterns the couple will dance, he must know the basic and a suitable variety of patterns in each dance.
2. He must maintain the proper dance frame for each dance.

3. He must keep time to the music which is one of the elements that keeps the couple synchronized. A man who dances off-time is very distracting and, consequently, difficult to follow.
4. He should lead with his body. Men used to be taught to lead with their hands, pushing and pulling their partners. This type of lead can be uncomfortable and looks awkward. Dancing should be pleasurable and appear effortless and smooth. Body leads are generally far more effective and attractive than hand leads.
5. The man should not depend upon verbal leads which are unnecessary.
6. The man is expected to begin each new pattern with his left foot.
7. He is also expected to finish whatever pattern he starts before moving on to a new pattern.
8. He must blend patterns smoothly so that one pattern flows easily into the next. Usually no one pattern should be repeated more than three times or the follower will become bored.
9. The leader should look ahead or where his toes are going. Looking at the feet can distort his body position and miscue the woman.
10. The man must follow line of dance and negotiate the traffic on the dance floor.

The woman's responsibilities:

1. The woman must know the basic step pattern in each dance.
2. She must maintain the proper dance frame without gap or air spaces through the forearms.
3. She must stay in time with the leader's body movements so the partners will move in unison.
4. She must maintain resistance or "be like a wall" for her partner, matching the amount of pressure he exerts. Women with no resistance, with "spaghetti" arms are difficult to lead, because there is no point of communication with them.
5. The woman should maintain her own balance at all times.
6. A good follower is patient. She should not anticipate the leaders's choices or "back lead" him. She should not move herself but rather should wait to be lead: It is true that in ballroom dance *only one can lead* and that lead belongs to the man.

7. The woman should be attentive to her partner's movements. She must concentrate on him and his leads. She should not focus on her feet because this can distract her attention from his leads.
8. The follower should be ready to move her right foot at the beginning of each pattern.
9. The woman should be responsive, ready to move once she sees and feels where her partner wants her to go. She should not lag behind or she will feel "heavy" and hard to lead.

There are three preliminary exercises that can help dancers learn to be good leaders and followers.

1. Elevator Exercise: Couples assume smooth closed position dance frame (p. 2). The woman closes her eyes and follows her partner as he rises to a stretched ankle position and then as he moves down to a bent knees lowered position. The leader should vary his speed and the follower should try to stay with him.
2. Walls: Partners place their arms up in the air as if they were told "stick 'em up" and they touch forearms. The man begins with his left foot and walks forward; the lady begins with her right foot and *when she feels his forward motion* starts to move backwards; she must wait for him to move her and must move with him! Partners can progress to walks done to music in even time (1-2, 1-2), with the feet brushing together on the "2" count.
3. Hook Exercise: Couples assume a swing open position (p. 7). Each exerts a small amount of resistance to the other, pulling back slightly until he feels his partner's force at the hand connection not in the elbows or shoulders (p. 101). Again using the hook as the point of connection, he takes a forward step using his body to move her one step back.

More than anything else, the leader must remember that whatever he does, will have an effect on his partner. She is attached to him; if he moves his hand or body, she is also moved.

Bad leads are leads that confuse the partner, leads that look bad and leads that hurt. Promenade, a widely danced pattern, is lead correctly with the man's head and shoulders; when he leads correctly, his shoulder will form a graceful long line extending across his back from elbow to elbow. But if the promenade is lead incorrectly, the man's top line can look broken and his shoulder blade can be pinched or his L arm can be too far extended because he has pulled the woman with his L hand making the couple look like a caricature of tango dancers, pointing their way down line of dance. When lead correctly, the woman will move slightly behind the man.

Good lead; dance
frame maintained

Good lead; long top
line

Bad lead: pinched
shoulder; dropped elbows

Bad lead: pulling and
pointing

Rhythm

> *As the drum beats, so goes the dance.* (Art 101 Limited dance poster)
> *Dancing is like robbing a bank. It takes split second timing.* (Art 101 Limited dance poster)

Dance is rhythm. Just as the heart keeps time for the human body, so, too, does the downbeat keep time for the dancer. How a couple look and feel on the dance floor depends upon the leader's ability to keep time to the music. Sadly, not everyone is born with an innate sense of rhythm, but rhythmic consciousness can be developed.

1. Listen to the music.
2. Feel the music, if possible, by pressing your hand flat on a speaker.
3. Clap the downbeat.
4. Clap the dance rhythm.
5. Be prepared to repeat this process often.
6. Become aware of music and try to find the downbeat whenever you hear music being played. The downbeat is usually marked by the percussive instruments (drums and piano) and/or the instruments playing the low part (bass and bass guitar).

Etiquette

Good dance manners are based on respect for other people and for their feelings. Dance egos are usually extremely fragile in the beginning. One must bear in mind that *"it takes two to tango."* (Al Hoffman and Dick Manning) Since ballroom dance is partner dance, the partners must remain aware of one another and try to create a supportive attitude. Accusations, insults and unsolicited dance instruction do not belong on the dance floor.

One asks for a dance by saying, "May I have this dance?" The invited partner should be escorted to and from the floor. If one refuses an invitation to dance, one should not dance the same dance with someone else! At the end of a dance both partners should thank one another.

It's usually considered impolite for everyone at a table to get up and dance, leaving one person behind. In a classroom setting no one person should be consistently left without a partner. Dancers should also make proper introductions of newcomers to acquaintances.

It's curious that very often dance egos grow from humble beginnings into monsters of enormous dimension. Some experienced dancers hog the dance floor giving unsolicited floor shows or trample beginning dancers and exhibit other kinds of prima donna behavior, all of which is rude and insufferable.

Good personal body hygiene and oral hygiene are strongly recommended due to the proximity of the partners. Appropriate dress is also important.

Good dance manners like good manners in other areas of life are based upon common sense and courtesy for fellow human beings. Putting oneself in the other person's shoes and taking time to be considerate will result in good manners.

ABBREVIATIONS AND SYMBOLS

and	dance on the half beat	**LOP**	left outside partner
br	brush	**nw**	no weight
bwd	backward	**op**	open position
CBMP	contrary body movement position	**opp**	opposite
ccw	counter clockwise	**p.**	page
chg	change	**pp.**	pages
cl	close	**PP**	promenade
cp	closed position	**Q**	quick
ct	count	**R**	turn right
cw	clockwise	**RF**	right foot
d	diagonal	**ROP**	right outside partner
dc	diagonal to center	**S**	slow
dr	draw	**sd**	side
dw	diagonal to wall	**sip**	step in place
fp	foot position	**tch**	touch
fwd	forward	**tog**	together
h	hold	**var**	variation
ip	in place	**wgt**	weight
L	turn left	**xib**	cross in back
LF	left foot	**xif**	cross in front
LOD	line of dance		

SMOOTH DANCES

Move Over Fred and Ginger

Among others, smooth dances include fox trot, waltz and tango. The object in these dances is to move or travel smoothly around the room, covering as much of the dance floor as possible. The couple should be streamlined, two people moving as one, gliding fluidly and forcefully around the dance floor; if they were dancing on water, there would be no ripples in their wake. Imagine a room filled with stiff whipped cream. The dancers' goal is to move smoothly and powerfully through the cream, charting a clean path without disrupting any of the cream around them.

To achieve this goal the couple must begin with good posture and a good dance frame (pp. 2–3). In my dance classes I play a game called statues. Couples dance 1 or 2 basic patterns to a song; each time I stop the music they must freeze and check their dance frames; they are asked to fix whatever is wrong and, then, when the music returns continue dancing. This game focuses attention on the dance frame and helps students to correct problems. Another technique is to dance using a practice dance hold. In this position the partners can't pull and push with his left arm and hand and her right arm and hand; this position also makes it easier to feel where the leader is travelling.

Practice dance hold—closed position

The leader must move with enough authority to move two people: himself and his partner. He leads with his chest and shoulders
taking long strides and propelling himself forward by using his back
leg as a powerhouse from which he pushes off. Each step starts with
a heel lead (as it would if he were walking down the street) and his
body weight is kept over the balls of his feet.

The follower waits until she feels the man move and then re-
sponds to his forward motion by reaching back from the hip. She
must think of pulling the thigh of her moving leg out of his way without allowing her derriere to stick out. To keep this from happening,
she needs to think of keeping her buttocks tucked underneath her
body or of keeping the thigh of her standing leg forward.

Incorrect reaching   Correct reaching

Sometimes partners will complain that they bump knees when
they dance. This happens because either one or both of them is moving from the knee rather than from the top of the leg. In the beginning
the women often complain that they're being trampled by the men.
This can happen because the woman is not keeping time with the
man, because her stride is too short or because she can't feel his lead,
due to her lack of resistance in her right hand or his lack of effective
lead.

One practice exercise which can help develop good smooth dance technique is to walk around the room with the thighs forward and buttocks tucked under on the inside edges of the feet. If nothing else, this provides good comic relief.

FOX TROT

History

The fox trot is no longer a trot at all, but rather a smooth, elegant dance. When watching couples gliding gracefully across the dance floor one doesn't think of the ragtime music that Harry Fox originally danced his now famous dance to in the 1914 Ziegfeld follies. The British dance masters smoothed away the trotting, hops and kicks when they imported the only smooth American ballroom dance to England and it is this smoother version which has endured over the years.

Rhythm

There are two different timings in fox trot: the patterns that fall into 8 counts or multiples of 4 counts and those that fall into 6 counts or multiples of 6 counts, the "magic" timing that Arthur Murray introduced.

Rhythm Time Signatures

Note that a 6 count pattern will require 1 1/2 measures of music and an 8 count pattern will require 2 measures of music.

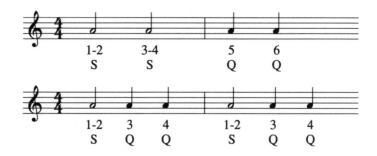

Frame

Fox trot is danced primarily in a closed dance position (pp. 2–3) using the hand holds shown on (p. 9). Keeping a good dance frame is essential for appearance and for successful leading and following.

Technique

The goal in fox trot is to move around the dance floor with long gliding perfectly smooth strides. Reread **Move Over Fred and Ginger** for specific suggestions that will aid in the successful accomplishment of the fox trot which is primarily a series of walks using various timing and positions.

Remember to keep both knees slightly relaxed at all times. On every second count in bronze fox trot the feet come together. Sometimes they will merely brush together and sometimes they will close together.

Parallel walks

Basic Forward Walk—Leader

Step	Foot & Direction	Degree & Direction of Turn	Rhythm	Musical Count	Comments
Facing LOD					
1	LF fwd		S	1–2	
2	RF fwd		S	3–4	
3	LF fwd		Q	5	
4	RF fwd		Q	6	

Note: Variations: A-Backing LOD move all the steps backward.
B-Steps 1–2 as above, step 3 LF sd, step 4 RF cl to LF.
C-Steps 1–2 as above, step 3 LF fwd ROP facing dc, step 4 RF fwd ROP facing dc. The man must move with enough authority to move two people; the lead is in his forward body motion; he must not let his lead fade on step 2 (ct 3–4) because this is the step which distinguishes the walk from the box.

Basic Forward Walk—Follower

Step	Foot & Direction	Degree & Direction of Turn	Rhythm	Musical Count	Comments
1	RF bwd		S	1–2	
2	LF bwd		S	3–4	
3	RF bwd		Q	5	
4	LF bwd		Q	6	

Note: Variations: A-Facing LOD move all the steps forward.
B-Steps 1–2 as above, step 3 RF sd, Step 4 LF cl to RF.
C-Steps 1–2 as above, step 3 RF bwd ROP backing dc, step 4 LF bwd ROP.

Promendade—Leader

Step	Foot & Direction	Degree & Direction of Turn	Rhythm	Musical Count	Comments
Facing Wall					
1	LF diag fwd	1/8 L	S	1–2	Man steps dw & sd under lady's elbow
2	RF fwd in CBMP		S	3–4	
3	LF sd	1/8 R	Q	5	
4	RF cl to LF		Q	6	

Note: See (p. 4) for dance frame and photo, and (pp. 19–20) for tips on leading and photos. An underarm turn R can be lead on the first of 2 successive promenades at steps 3 and 4; the man raises his L arm to lead; there is no turn on the second promenade.

Promenade—Follower

Step	Foot & Direction	Degree & Direction of Turn	Rhythm	Musical Count	Comments
1	RF diag bwd & sd	1/8 R	S	1–2	Lady steps slightly behind the man
2	LF fwd in CBMP		S	3–4	
3	RF sd	1/8 R	Q	5	
4	LF cl to RF		Q	6	

Note: (See pp. 4, 19–20.) In the underarm turn the woman makes a progressive pivot turn and "spots" (p. 135) down LOD to avoid dizziness.

Parallel Walks—Leader

Step	Foot & Direction	Degree & Direction of Turn	Rhythm	Musical Count	Comments
Facing Wall					
1	LF fwd dw	1/8 L	S	1–2	ROP
2	RF fwd in CBMP		S	3–4	ROP
3	LF sd	1/4 R	Q	5	LOP
4	RF cl to LF		Q	6	LOP
5	LF bwd backing dc		S	1–2	LOP
6	RF bwd		S	3–4	LOP
7	LF sd dw	1/4 L	Q	5	ROP
8	RF cl to LF		Q	6	ROP

Note: In ROP and LOP partners will overlap right sides of bodies and left sides of bodies. To lead the gentleman turns with authority stepping under the lady's R elbow. See (p. 5) for ROP.

Parallel Walks—Follower

Step	Foot & Direction	Degree & Direction of Turn	Rhythm	Musical Count	Comments
1	RF bwd	1/8 L	S	1–2	ROP
2	LF bwd		S	3–4	ROP
3	RF sd	1/4 R	Q	5	LOP
4	LF cl to RF		Q	6	LOP
5	RF fwd		S	1–2	LOP
6	LF fwd		S	3–4	LOP
7	RF sd	1/4 L	Q	5	ROP
8	LF cl to RF		Q	6	ROP

Walks with 1/4 Turns—Leader

Step	Foot & Direction	Degree & Direction of Turn	Rhythm	Musical Count	Comments
Facing dw					
1	LF fwd		S	1–2	
2	RF fwd	1/4 R	S	3–4	
3	LF sd		Q	5	
4	RF cl to LF		Q	6	
Backing dc					
5	LF bwd		S	1–2	
6	RF bwd	1/4 L	S	3–4	
7	LF sd		Q	5	
8	RF cl to LF		Q	6	

Note: This pattern can be danced outside partner—on step 2 leader steps ROP in CBMP beginning his 1/4 turn R; on step 6 leader steps LOP in CBMP beginning his 1/4 turn L.

Walks with 1/4 Turns—Follower

Step	Foot & Direction	Degree & Direction of Turn	Rhythm	Musical Count	Comments
1	RF bwd		S	1–2	
2	LF bwd	1/4 R	S	3–4	
3	RF sd		Q	5	
4	LF cl to RF		Q	6	
5	RF fwd		S	1–2	
6	LF fwd		S	3–4	
7	RF sd	1/4 L	Q	5	
8	LF cl to RF		Q	6	

Left Turn—Leader

Step	Foot & Direction	Degree & Direction of Turn	Rhythm	Musical Count	Comments
1	LF fwd	1/8 L	Q	1	
2	RF tch LF		Q	2	
3	RF bwd	1/8 L	Q	3	
4	LF tch RF		Q	4	
5	LF sd		Q	5	
6	RF cl to LF		Q	6	

Note: The man leads by turning his body and stepping directly into the woman on step 1.

Left Turn—Follower

Step	Foot & Direction	Degree & Direction of Turn	Rhythm	Musical Count	Comments
1	RF bwd	1/8 L	Q	1	
2	LF tch RF		Q	2	
3	LF fwd	1/8 L	Q	3	
4	RF tch LF		Q	4	
5	RF sd		Q	5	
6	LF cl to RF		Q	6	

Left Box—Leader

Step	Foot & Direction	Degree & Direction of Turn	Rhythm	Musical Count	Comments
Facing LOD					
1	LF fwd		S	1–2	ct 2 RF br LF
2	RF sd	1/4 L	Q	3	
3	LF cl to RF		Q	4	
4	RF bwd		S	5–6	ct 6 LF br RF
5	LF sd	1/4 L	Q	7	
6	RF cl to LF		Q	8	
7–12	Repeat 1–6 end facing LOD				

Note: On counts 2 and 6 the feet brush together. The man leads the turn with his upper body by turning his own head and shoulders as he steps.
Note: On counts 2 and 6 the feet brush together.

Left Box—Follower

Step	Foot & Direction	Degree & Direction of Turn	Rhythm	Musical Count	Comments
1	RF bwd		S	1–2	ct 2 LF br RF
2	LF sd	1/4 L	Q	3	
3	RF cl to LF		Q	4	
4	LF fwd		S	5–6	ct 6 RF br LF
5	RF sd	1/4 L	Q	7	
6	LF cl to RF		Q	8	
7–12	Repeat 1–6				

Forward Boxes—Leader

Step	Foot & Direction	Degree & Direction of Turn	Rhythm	Musical Count	Comments
Facing LOD					
1	LF fwd		S	1–2	ct 2 RF br LF
2	RF sd		Q	3	
3	LF cl to RF		Q	4	
4	RF fwd		S	5–6	ct 6 LF br RF
5	LF sd		Q	7	
6	RF cl to LF		Q	8	

Forward Boxes—Follower

Step	Foot & Direction	Degree & Direction of Turn	Rhythm	Musical Count	Comments
1	RF bwd		S	1–2	ct 2 LF br RF
2	LF sd		Q	3	
3	RF cl to LF		Q	4	
4	LF bwd		S	5–6	ct 6 RF br LF
5	RF sd		Q	7	
6	LF cl to RF		Q	8	

Forward & Back Boxes—Leader

Step	Foot & Direction	Degree & Direction of Turn	Rhythm	Musical Count	Comments
Begin diagonal wall					
1	LF fwd		S	1–2	ct 2 RF br LF
2	RF sd		Q	3	
3	LF cl to RF		Q	4	
4	RF fwd	1/4 R	S	1–2	ct 2 LF br RF
5	LF sd		Q	3	
6	RF cl to LF		Q	4	
7	LF bwd		S	1–2	ct 2 RF br LF
8	RF sd		Q	3	
9	LF cl to RF		Q	4	
10	RF bwd	1/4 L	S	1–2	ct 2 LF br RF
11	LF sd		Q	3	
12	RF cl to LF		Q	4	

Note: On ct 2 the feet brush together. This pattern moves on the diagonals (p. 15). The man leads the turn on step 4 with his head and body stepping directly into or through his partner. The lady leads steps 7–10.

Forward & Back Boxes—Follower

Step	Foot & Direction	Degree & Direction of Turn	Rhythm	Musical Count	Comments
Begin diagonal wall					
1	RF bwd		S	1–2	ct 2 LF br RF
2	LF sd		Q	3	
3	RF cl to LF		Q	4	
4	LF bwd	1/4 R	S	1–2	ct 2 RF br LF
5	RF sd		Q	3	
6	LF cl to RF		Q	4	
7	RF fwd		S	1–2	ct 2 LF br RF
8	LF sd		Q	3	
9	RF cl to LF		Q	4	
10	LF fwd	1/4 L	S	1–2	ct 2 RF br LF
11	RF sd		Q	3	
12	LF cl to RF		Q	4	

Right Box—Leader

Step	Foot & Direction	Degree & Direction of Turn	Rhythm	Musical Count	Comments
Facing LOD					
Steps 1–3 of Forward Boxes					
4	RF fwd	1/4 R	S	5–6	ct 6 LF br RF
5	LF sd		Q	7	
6	RF cl to LF		Q	8	
7	LF bwd	1/4 R	S	1–2	ct 2 RF br RF
8	RF sd		Q	3	
9	LF cl to RF		Q	4	
10–15 Repeat 4–9 end facing LOD					
Steps 4–6 of Forward Boxes					

Note: On counts 2 and 6 the feet brush together. The man leads the turn by turning his head and shoulders R as he steps.

Right Box—Follower

Step	Foot & Direction	Degree & Direction of Turn	Rhythm	Musical Count	Comments
Steps 1–3 of Forward Boxes					
4	LF bwd		S	5–6	ct 6 RF br LF
5	RF sd	1/4 R	Q	7	
6	LF cl to RF		Q	8	
7	RF fwd		S	1–2	ct 2 LF br RF
8	LF sd	1/4 R	Q	3	
9	RF cl to LF		Q	4	
10–15 Repeat 4–9					
Steps 4–6 of Forward Boxes					

Note: On counts 2 and 6 the feet brush together.

Left and Right Boxes

These can be combined beginning with the Left Box, then adding the Right box and then starting again with the Left Box, etc. . . . The dancers make 1/4 turns.

A more advanced version increases the amount of turn and changes the direction of movement to dance the diagonals.

Advanced Left and Right Boxes—Leader

Step	Foot & Direction	Degree & Direction of Turn	Rhythm	Musical Count	Comments
Begin diagonal center					
1	LF fwd		S	1–2	ct 2 RF br LF
2	RF sd	3/8 L	Q	3	
3	LF cl to RF		Q	4	
Backing LOD					
4	RF bwd		S	5–6	ct 6 LF br RF
5	LF sd	3/8 L	Q	7	L toe points dw
6	RF cl to LF		Q	8	
Facing diagonal wall					
7	LF fwd		S	1–2	ct 2 RF br LF
8	RF sd		Q	3	
9	LF cl to RF		Q	4	
10	RF fwd	3/8 R	S	5–6	ct 6 LF br RF
11	LF sd		Q	7	
12	RF cl to LF		Q	8	
Backing LOD					
13	LF bwd		S	1–2	ct 2 RF br LF
14	RF sd	3/8 R	Q	3	R toe points dc
15	LF cl to RF		Q	4	
Facing diagonal center					
16	RF fwd		S	5–6	ct 6 LF br RF
17	LF sd		Q	7	
18	RF cl to LF		Q	8	

Advanced Left and Right Boxes—Follower

Step	Foot & Direction	Degree & Direction of Turn	Rhythm	Musical Count	Comments
1	RF bwd		S	1–2	ct 2 LF br RF
2	LF sd	3/8 L	Q	3	
3	RF cl to LF		Q	4	
4	LF fwd		S	5–6	ct 6 RF br LF
5	RF sd	3/8 L	Q	7	
6	LF cl to RF		Q	8	
7	RF bwd		S	1–2	ct 2 LF br RF
8	LF sd		Q	3	
9	RF cl to LF		Q	4	
10	LF bwd		S	5–6	ct 6 RF br LF
11	RF sd	3/8 R	Q	7	
12	LF cl to RF		Q	8	
13	RF fwd		S	1–2	ct 2 LF br RF
14	LF sd	3/8 R	Q	3	
15	RF cl to LF		Q	4	
16	LF bwd		S	5–6	ct 6 RF br LF
17	RF sd		Q	7	
18	LF cl to RF		Q	8	

WALTZ

History

Waltz, whose home was Germany, was also popular in Austria and Switzerland. It is the oldest of the ballroom dances, dating from the middle of the eighteenth century. Its roots are in folk dancing and it is both a dance of the people and a dance of polite society. Today it is hard to imagine that the close hold which it required created quite a controversy when it was first introduced. Napoleon's invading soldiers spread the waltz from Germany to Paris; then the dance glided across the channel to England and finally made its way to the United States. Today both the faster Viennese Waltz, made forever popular by the Strauss family, and the slower English style waltz are extremely popular with dancers of all ages.

Rhythm

There are no "slows" and "quicks" in waltz. The time is 3/4 time with three beats per measure. The accent is on the "2" count and this count is drawn out as long as possible.

Rhythm Time Signature

Frame

Waltz is danced primarily in a closed dance position (pp. 2–3) using the hand holds shown on (p. 9). Keeping a good dance frame is essential for appearance and for successful leading and following.

Technique

Reread **Move Over Fred and Ginger** for specific suggestions that will aid in the successful accomplishment of this continuously flowing dance. The rhythmically lilting quality of the waltz derives from the sway and the rise and fall. The sway is used on turning patterns and requires a slight inclination of the body to the left when stepping with the left foot and to the right when stepping with the right foot. The rise and fall begin with a slight lowering through the standing leg on the "and" count; then there is a swinging forward (as if on a rope swing sailing out over a lake). On the "2" count, there is a rise using ankle stretch with knees bent and thighs forward; on the "3" count, the feet are together. The knees remain slightly bent even in the full rise position. The lowering must be through the standing or supporting leg only; lowering through the leg that the dancer is travelling to will result in a grotesque bumpy lunge. The lowering is used by the couple as a period of "collecting" or a time for synchronizing their movements. Couples can practice this by taking closed dance position, having the follower close her eyes as the leader pretends to be an elevator rising and falling with feet slightly apart and thighs forward. The leader can vary his tempo as the follower tries to match his movements.

Lower through the standing leg

Ankle stretch, thighs forward, knees bent

Left Box—Leader

Step	Foot & Direction	Degree & Direction of Turn	Musical Count	Comments
Facing LOD				
1	LF fwd		1	Sway left
2	RF sd	1/4 L	2	
3	LF cl to RF		3	
4	RF bwd		4	Sway right
5	LF sd	1/4 L	5	
6	RF cl to LF		6	
7–12	Repeat 1–6 end facing LOD			

Note: The man leads the turn with his upper body by turning his own head and shoulders as he steps. The foot placement is like that of fox trot and rumba, but the counts are different.

Left Box—Follower

Step	Foot & Direction	Degree & Direction of Turn	Musical Count	Comments
1	RF bwd		1	Sway right
2	LF sd	1/4 L	2	
3	RF cl to LF		3	
4	LF bwd		4	Sway left
5	RF sd	1/4 L	5	
6	LF cl to RF		6	
7–12	Repeat 1–6			

Note: The man leads the turn with his upper body by turning his own head and shoulders as he steps. The foot placement is like that of fox trot and rumba, but the counts are different.

Forward Boxes—Leader

Step	Foot & Direction	Degree & Direction of Turn	Musical Count	Comments
Facing LOD				
1	LF fwd		1	
2	RF sd		2	
3	LF cl to RF		3	
4	RF fwd		4	
5	LF sd		5	
6	RF cl to LF		6	

Forward Boxes—Follower

Step	Foot & Direction	Degree & Direction of Turn	Musical Count	Comments
1	RF bwd		1	
2	LF sd		2	
3	RF cl to LF		3	
4	LF bwd		4	
5	RF sd		5	
6	LF cl to RF		6	

Forward & Back Boxes—Leader

Step	Foot & Direction	Degree & Direction of Turn	Rhythm	Musical Count	Comments
Begin diagonal wall					
1	LF fwd			1	
2	RF sd			2	
3	LF cl to RF			3	
4	RF fwd	1/4 R		4	
5	LF sd			5	
6	RF cl to LF			6	
7	LF bwd			1	
8	RF sd			2	
9	LF cl to RF			3	
10	RF bwd	1/4 L		4	
11	LF sd			5	
12	RF cl to LF			6	

Note: This pattern moves on the diagonals (p. 15). The man leads the turn on step 4 with his head and body stepping directly into or through his partner. The lady leads steps 7–10.

Forward & Back Boxes—Follower

Step	Foot & Direction	Degree & Direction of Turn	Rhythm	Musical Count	Comments
1	RF bwd			1	
2	LF sd			2	
3	RF cl to LF			3	
4	LF bwd	1/4 R		4	
5	RF sd			5	
6	LF cl to RF			6	
7	RF fwd			1	
8	LF sd			2	
9	RF cl to LF			3	
10	LF fwd	1/4 L		4	
11	RF sd			5	
12	LF cl to RF			6	

Right Box—Leader

Step	Foot & Direction	Degree & Direction of Turn	Musical Count	Comments
Facing LOD				
Steps 1–3 of Forward Boxes				
4	RF fwd		4	Sway right
5	LF sd	1/4 R	5	
6	RF cl to LF		6	
7	LF bwd		1	Sway left
8	RF sd	1/4 R	2	
9	LF cl to RF		3	
10–15	Repeat 4–9, end facing LOD			
Steps 4–6 of Forward boxes				

Note: The man leads the turn by turning his head and shoulders R as he steps.

Right Box—Follower

Step	Foot & Direction	Degree & Direction of Turn	Musical Count	Comments
Steps 1–3 of Forward Boxes				
4	LF bwd		4	Sway left
5	RF sd	1/4 R	5	
6	LF cl to RF		6	
7	RF fwd		1	Sway right
8	LF sd	1/4 R	2	
9	RF cl to LF		3	
10–15	Repeat 4–9			
Steps 4–6 of Forward boxes				

Left and Right Boxes

The boxes can be combined beginning with the Left Box; then adding the Right Box and then starting again with the Left Box, etc. . . . The dancers make 1/4 turns.

A more advanced version increases the amount of turn and changes the direction of movement.

Advanced Left and Right Boxes—Leader

Step	Foot & Direction	Degree & Direction of Turn	Musical Count	Comments
Begin diagonal center				
1	LF fwd		1	Sway left
2	RF sd	3/8 L	2	
3	LF cl to RF		3	
Backing LOD				
4	RF bwd		4	Sway right
5	LF sd	3/8 L	5	L toe points dw
6	RF cl to LF		6	
Facing diagonal wall				
7	LF fwd		1	
8	RF sd		2	
9	LF cl to RF		3	
10	RW fwd		4	Sway right
11	LF sd	3/8 R	5	
12	RF cl to LF		6	
Backing LOD				
13	LF bwd		1	Sway left
14	RF sd	3/8 R	2	R toe points dc
15	LF cl to RF		3	
Facing diagonal center				
16	RF fwd		4	
17	LF sd		5	
18	RF cl to LF		6	

Advanced Left and Right Boxes—Follower

Step	Foot & Direction	Degree & Direction of Turn	Musical Count	Comments
1	RF bwd		1	Sway right
2	LF sd	3/8 L	2	
3	RF cl to LF		3	
4	LF fwd		4	Sway left
5	RF sd	3/8 L	5	
6	LF cl to RF		6	
7	RF bwd		1	
8	LF sd		2	
9	RF cl to LF		3	
10	LF bwd		4	Sway left
11	RF sd	3/8 R	5	
12	LF cl to RF		6	
13	RF fwd		1	Sway right
14	LF sd	3/8 R	2	
15	RF cl to LF		3	
16	LF bwd		4	
17	RF sd		5	
18	LF cl to RF		6	

Forward hesitation

Forward and Back Hesitation—Leader

Step	Foot & Direction	Degree & Direction of Turn	Musical Count	Comments
1	LF fwd		1	
2	RF cl to LF nw		2	Rise as RF touches
			3	Hold
3	RF bwd		4	
4	LF cl to RF nw		5	Rise as LF touches
			6	Hold

Note: The lead is the rise which comes a little earlier than usual. Sometimes dancers will change weight on counts 2 and 3 while remaining in place, i.e., fwd, change, weight, back, change, weight. Some dancers even use this as a waltz basic calling it the "valse a deux temps" or the "hesitation waltz." It is an excellent way to teach waltz to children aged 5–9.

Forward and Back Hesitation—Follower

Step	Foot & Direction	Degree & Direction of Turn	Musical Count	Comments
1	RF bwd		1	
2	LF cl to RF nw		2	Rise as LF touches
			3	Hold
3	LF fwd		4	
4	RF cl to LF nw		5	Rise as RF touches
			6	Hold

Note: See leader's note.

Left Hesitation Turn—Leader

Step	Foot & Direction	Degree & Direction of Turn	Musical Count	Comments
1	LF fwd		1	
2	RF cl to LF nw		2	Rise as RF touches
			3	Hold
3	RF bwd		4	
4	LF sd	1/4 L	5	
5	RF cl to LF		6	

Note: The man leads the turn on count 4 by turning his shoulders as he steps back.

Left Hesitation Turn—Follower

Step	Foot & Direction	Degree & Direction of Turn	Musical Count	Comments
1	RF bwd		1	
2	LF cl to RF nw		2	Rise as LF touches
			3	Hold
3	LF fwd		4	
4	RF sd	1/4 L	5	
5	LF cl to RF		6	

Note: The woman follows the man's shoulders, stepping right into him on count 4.

Parallel Walks—Leader

Step	Foot & Direction	Degree & Direction of Turn	Musical Count	Comments
Facing Wall				
1	LF fwd dw	1/8 L	1	ROP
2	RF fwd		2	ROP
3	LF fwd		3	ROP
4	RF fwd in CBMP		4	
5	LF sd backing dc ⌝	1/4 R	5	
6	RF cl to LF ⌟		6	
7	LF bwd		1	LOP
8	RF bwd		2	LOP
9	LF bwd		3	LOP
10	RF bwd in CBMP		4	
11	LF sd ⌝	1/4 L	5	
12	RF cl to LF ⌟		6	

Note: See (p. 5) for photo of ROP. In ROP and LOP partners will overlap right sides of bodies and left sides of bodies. To lead, the gentleman turns with authority stepping under the lady's R elbow.

Parallel Walks—Follower

Step	Foot & Direction	Degree & Direction of Turn	Musical Count	Comments
1	RF bwd	1/8 L	1	ROP
2	LF bwd		2	ROP
3	RF bwd		3	ROP
4	LF bwd		4	
5	RF sd ⌝	1/4 R	5	
6	LF cl to RF ⌟		6	
7	RF fwd		1	LOP
8	LF fwd		2	LOP
9	RF fwd		3	LOP
10	LF fwd		4	
11	RF sd ⌝	1/4 L	5	
12	LF cl to RF ⌟		6	

TANGO

History

The deep roots of tango lie in African slavery for tango is a mixture of dances peculiar to Blacks in Haiti, Cuba and Argentina. Both the music and the dance were intense and erotic; perhaps this is why they became popular in the nightclubs of Buenos Aries. In 1907 the dance was introduced in France; by 1912 it crossed the channel to England. The dance was so popular in France and England that tango teas became the rage. It was danced in the United States first by the Castles and then by the movie star, Rudolph Valentino. The broadway show, *Tango Argentino,* helped to rekindle enthusiasm for this exciting, sensual dance.

Rhythm

Tango music varies somewhat in style and tempo depending upon whether it is designed for International style, American style or authentic Argentine tango as it is danced by Argentines.

Rhythm Time Signatures

The tango basic step uses 2 measures or 8 counts of music.

1-2	3-4	5	6	7-8
S	S	Q	Q	S

Frame

Tango also uses the closed dance position (pp. 2–3) but the lady's left hand position differs from fox trot and waltz. Her thumb is spread underneath the man's underarm while her fingers extend along his back. (p. 9.) The couple must maintain a good dance frame to be successful at leading and following this expressive dance.

Technique

The image so often associated with tango is that of a cat stalking its prey. This is, however, no tame pussycat; imagine the sensual movement of a wild tiger and you begin to approximate the correct movement. Tango is not as flowing as fox trot or waltz; it has an intense staccato quality that makes it unique. It is a dance of stops. There is a crisp placement of the feet combined with a driving body movement so that the body moves and then the feet seem to check that movement. Yet it is a smooth, fluid dance and all of the suggestions given in **Move Over Fred and Ginger** will be helpful in achieving proper technique. The knees should be slightly more flexed than for other smooth dances and should remain flexed. There is no sway or rise and fall in tango; the shoulders should be kept level at all times.

Basic—Leader

Step	Foot & Direction	Degree & Direction of Turn	Rhythm	Musical Count	Comments
1	LF fwd		S	1–2	
2	RF fwd		S	3–4	
3	LF fwd		Q	5	Sometimes called a "Tan-go close;" frequently ends patterns
4	RF sd		Q	6	
5	LF cl to RF nw		S	7–8	

Basic—Follower

Step	Foot & Direction	Degree & Direction of Turn	Rhythm	Musical Count	Comments
1	RF bwd		S	1–2	
2	LF bwd		S	3–4	
3	RF bwd		Q	5	
4	LF sd		Q	6	
5	RF cl to LF nw		S	7–8	

Parallel Walk—Leader

Step	Foot & Direction	Degree & Direction of Turn	Rhythm	Musical Count	Comments
1	LF fwd dc	1/8 L	S	1–2	
2	RF fwd in CBMP		S	3–4	ROP
3	LF fwd		Q	5	
4	RF sd		Q	6	
5	LF cl to RF nw		S	7–8	

Parallel Walk—Follower

Step	Foot & Direction	Degree & Direction of Turn	Rhythm	Musical Count	Comments
1	RF bwd	1/8 L	S	1–2	
2	LF bwd in CBMP		S	3–4	ROP
3	RF bwd		Q	5	
4	LF sd		Q	6	
5	RF cl to LF nw		S	7–8	

Promenade—Leader

Step	Foot & Direction	Degree & Direction of Turn	Rhythm	Musical Count	Comments
Facing Wall					
1	LF fwd dw	1/8 L	S	1–2	
2	RF fwd in CBMP		S	3–4	
3	LF fwd		Q	5	
4	RF sd		Q	6	
5	LF cl to RF nw		S	7–8	

Note: See (p. 4) for dance frame and photo and (pp. 19–20) for tips on leading and photos.

Promenade—Follower

Step	Foot & Direction	Degree & Direction of Turn	Rhythm	Musical Count	Comments
1	RF bwd and slightly sd	1/8 R	S	1–2	
2	LF fwd in CBMP		S	3–4	
3	RF bwd	1/8 L	Q	5	
4	LF sd		Q	6	
5	RF cl to LF nw		S	7–8	

Note: See (p. 4) for dance frame and photo and (pp. 19–20) for tips on leading and photos.

Rock and Corte—Leader

Step	Foot & Direction	Degree & Direction of Turn	Rhythm	Musical Count	Comments
1	LF fwd		Q	1	⎤ Rock
2	RF bwd and sd		Q	2	⎦
3	LF bwd		S	3–4	
4	RF fwd		S	1–2	
5–8	Repeat 1–4				
9	LF fwd		Q	1	
10	RF sd		Q	2	
11	LF cl to RF nw		S	3–4	

Note: This pattern looks nice with 1/8 turns L on steps 1, 2, 5 and 6. On steps 3 and 7 the man must keep his back straight, his R foot on the ground with straight R leg and bent L knee.

Rock and Corte—Follower

Step	Foot & Direction	Degree & Direction of Turn	Rhythm	Musical Count	Comments
1	RF bwd		Q	1	⎤ Rock
2	LF fwd and sd		Q	2	⎦
3	RF fwd		S	3–4	
4	LF bwd		S	1–2	
5–8	Repeat 1–4				
9	RF bwd		Q	1	
10	LF sd		Q	2	
11	RF cl to LF nw		S	3–4	

Note: See leader's note. On steps 3 and 7 the woman bends her R knee, straightens her L leg pushing down her L heel as she "turns out" the L leg; her upper body must be erect or "pulled up". Her eyes look over her L elbow.

Proper corte line   La Puerta: woman   La Puerta: woman
                     fans; leg on floor   fans; leg raised

La Puerta—Leader

Step	Foot & Direction	Degree & Direction of Turn	Rhythm	Musical Count	Comments
1	LF fwd	1/8 L	Q	1	⌉ Rock
2	RF bwd and sd	1/8 L	Q	2	⌡
3	RF bwd in CBMP		S	⌈ 3	ROP
4	dr RF to xif LF			⌐ 4	ROP
5	RF fwd in CBMP		S	⌊ 1	PP
6	RF ip			2	CP
7–12	Repeat 1–6				
13	LF fwd		Q	1	
14	RF sd		Q	2	
15	LF cl to RF nw		S	3–4	

Note: The woman fans on steps 3–6. The man must not attempt to push the woman with his hands or arms into the ROP and PP fans. As always his body leads hers.

La Puerta—Follower

Step	Foot & Direction	Degree & Direction of Turn	Rhythm	Musical Count	Comments
1	RF bwd	1/8 L	Q	1 ⎤	Rock
2	LF fwd and sd		Q	2	
3	RF fwd in CBMP		S	⎡ 3	ROP Release heel;
4	RF sip	3/8 R		⎣ 4	pivot on ball of RF ending PP
5	LF fwd in CBMP		S	⎡ 1	Release heel; pivot on ball
6	LF sip	3/8 L		⎣ 2	of LF ending CP
7–12	Repeat 1–6				
13	RF bwd		Q	1	
14	LF sd		Q	2	
15	RF cl to LF nw		S	3–4	

Note: The woman can fan (step 4) by keeping her L leg on the floor behind her with her heel pressed down and weight on the inside edge of the L ball or she can bend the L leg at the knee keeping the lower leg parallel to the floor. See photos (p. 56). On step 6 she can fan the R leg using either of the 2 previously described leg positions or using a hook where she rests the R insole on the heel of the L foot so that the inside edge of the R ankle presses against the back of the L ankle in a modified third foot position.

RHYTHM DANCES

Fast and Fun

These dances are not the dignified ballroom dances, although once refined, many of them are performed in ballroom dance competitions. These are the more primal dances, the dances of the people, the dances of the streets, the dance crazes like the charleston, lindy, cha-cha, jitterbug, disco or Texas two-step. These dances are usually "hot" and they're always fun. They tend to be "spot" dances, that is, their dancers usually stay in one area of the dance floor versus travelling around the room.

Rhythm dance music is usually foot stomping or at the very least toe-tapping or finger-snapping music; it shouts out in the words of the 60's song, *dance to the music.* (Sly and the Family Stone) It is usually up-tempo and marked by a strong simple rhythm. Very often this rhythm finds expression in the dancer's body through a relaxing and straightening of the knees and a movement of the hips. Generally the shoulders are quiet. The steps taken in rhythm dances are much smaller than the steps of smooth dances. Remember the famous dance proverb, *the faster the music, the smaller the step.*

The follower does a lot of turning in rhythm dances and it is important that she learns to stand tall, imagining that she has a pole going through the center of her body as she turns. Since the head of the body is the heaviest body part, looking down in a turn will pull the entire body off balance; eyes need to stay at eye level. Spotting, a technique used to prevent dizziness, requires that the turner focuses on an imaginary or real object at eye level; this focus point is the only thing seen during the rotation (p. 135). To avoid hitting the leader with her elbow, the follower must remember to keep her right elbow in a straight vertical line under her wrist when executing underarm turns.

Jitterbug

The leads still originate in the man's lower body but are sometimes communicated through his hands and arms. The dance posture is still very upright and the dancers must still *come to dance*. They can imagine that they have two headlights placed just above the woman's upper anatomy (or man's) and they should allow their lights to shine out like lighthouse beacons. They never want to turn their lights downward. The weight is still kept forward over the balls of the feet and the footwork is still sharp and precise. The dancers should feel the floor in swing, samba and the three Cuban dances and they should have a sense of pushing heavily into the floor. Polka is, however, somewhat lighter.

LATIN DANCES

Under Latin dances I have grouped the Cuban rumba, mambo, and cha-cha as well as the Brazilian samba. What these dances have in common is their Latin American origin and Black African roots. The body motion of the samba is, however, different from the "Cuban motion" of the big three Cuban dances.

The "Cuban" hip motion occurs between the ribs and the knees with the shoulders held silent. The hip action mimics that which occurs naturally when one walks up a set of stairs. Next time you walk up a set of stairs, pay close attention to what your hips are doing. The knees bend and straighten alternately; the bent knee is weighted, and as the knee straightens, the weight is transferred to the other leg. One of the easiest ways to learn the hip motion is to hold onto the shoulders or hips of someone who has mastered the hip action and follow his movements. In my classes we make cha-cha choo choos, long single file lines of dancers each holding on to the shoulders or hips of the person in front. We practice taking steps to the left, right, forward and backward using hip motion; then we practice the basic. Sometimes over zealous dancers will start to work too hard at the hip motion and get an unsightly "grinding" of the hips; Cuban motion is fluid, soft and sexy, not forced.

The hips are soft in Latin dance, but the feet are precise, even staccato or knife-like. The dancer should begin in a slightly turned out first foot position squeezing the knees together and rolled to the inside edges of the feet. Every subsequent step should be taken with ankle stretch on the inside edges of the feet. A pretty leg line is obtained by keeping the feet slightly turned out with one leg "covering" the other during the forward and back steps. Be sure not to shuffle the feet, but rather to work the whole foot with each step and to stretch the ankles.

Latin leg line

Stepping onto the inside edge of the foot

Teepee: practice
Latin hold

Rounded Latin dance frame

The dance frame is more rounded than the closed dance position. See (pp. 6 & 10) for photos and suggestions. Sometimes, when I am first teaching mambo or cha-cha, I will ask my students to practice their basic step in a teepee position. This helps dancers keep their weight forward over the balls of their feet and helps them to feel their partner's forward motion.

RUMBA

History

This erotic sensual dance originated in Cuba and combined African and Cuban rhythms. It reached the United States in the late 1920's.

Rhythm

American style rumba has a hold on the "2" count; the foot does not move although there is a hip change. There is a break step on counts "3" and "4" with hip changes on each count. This is the slowest of the three Cuban dances.

Rhythm Time Signatures

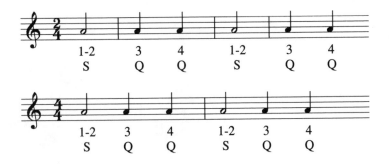

Frame

The Latin dance frame which has been discussed on (pp. 6 & 10) is used.

Technique

Reread **Latin Dance** for a description of proper technique. Other suggestions are given in **Rhythm Dance.** Keep the hips soft and fluid.

Left Box—Leader

Step	Foot & Direction	Degree & Direction of Turn	Rhythm	Musical Count	Comments
1	LF fwd		S	1–2	Shift hip on ct 2
2	RF sd	1/4 L	Q	3	
3	LF cl to RF		Q	4	
4	RF bwd		S	5–6	Shift hip on ct 6
5	LF sd	1/4 L	Q	7	
6	RF cl to LF		Q	8	
7–12 Repeat 1–6					

Left Box—Follower

Step	Foot & Direction	Degree & Direction of Turn	Rhythm	Musical Count	Comments
1	RF bwd		S	1–2	Shift hip on ct 2
2	LF sd	1/4 L	Q	3	
3	RF cl to LF		Q	4	
4	LF fwd		S	5–6	Shift hip on ct 6
5	RF sd	1/4 L	Q	7	
6	LF cl to RF		Q	8	
7–12 Repeat 1–6					

Crossover—Leader

Step	Foot & Direction	Degree & Direction of Turn	Rhythm	Musical Count	Comments
1	LF fwd		S	1–2	
2	RF sd		Q	3	
3	LF cl to RF		Q	4	
4	RF sd		S	5–6	
5	LF fwd	1/4 R	Q	7	Release heel of RF; pivot on ball
6	RF sip		Q	8	
7	LF sd	1/4 L	S	1–2	
8	RF fwd	1/4 L	Q	3	Release heel of LF; pivot on ball
9	LF sip		Q	4	
10–15	Repeat 4–9 with 1/4 turn R on step 4				
16	RF sd	1/4 R	S	5–6	Take lady back into closed Latin dance position
17	LF cl to RF		Q	7	
18	RF cl to LF		Q	8	

Note: On step 4 (ct 6) the man changes to a pistol hand hold (p. 10). On step 5 (ct 7) he draws the lady into a crossover; they are forearm to forearm through the middle; his right arm and her left are extended making sure that the arms remain soft at the elbows and in front of their bodies; their hands have thumbs down and knuckles forward. The feet are turned out in a 5th foot position (p. 8) with the front toe pointing toward partner and the back foot away from partner. The man's L side and woman's R side are lifted to help create a pretty line. This procedure is repeated on the opposite side. A walk around turn may be done by both partners as an alternative ending.

Crossover—Follower

Step	Foot & Direction	Degree & Direction of Turn	Rhythm	Musical Count	Comments
1	RF bwd		S	1–2	
2	LF sd		Q	3	
3	RF cl to LF		Q	4	
4	LF sd		S	5–6	
5	RF fwd	1/4 L	Q	7	Release heel of LF; pivot on ball
6	LF sip		Q	8	
7	RF sd	1/4 R	S	1–2	
8	LF fwd	1/4 R	Q	3	Release heel of RF; pivot on ball
9	RF sip		Q	4	
10–12	Repeat 4–6 with 1/4 turn L on step 4				
13–15	Repeat 7–9				
16	LF sd	1/4 L	S	5–6	
17	RF cl to LF		Q	7	
18	LF cl to RF		Q	8	

Note: See leader's note.

Crossover

Walk-Around Turn—Leader

Step	Foot & Direction	Degree & Direction of Turn	Rhythm	Musical Count	Comments
Steps 1–12 crossover					
13	LF sd		S	1–2	
14	RF fwd	1/2 L	Q	3	About face on
15	LF sip	1/2 L	Q	4	steps 14 & 15 turn first, then step
16	RF sd	1/4 L	S	5–6	
17	LF cl to RF		Q	7	
18	RF cl to LF		Q	8	

Note: Use spotting on the turn; make it clean and crisp. Allow the body (through spotting) to move the foot. Lead with the R hand on step 13 (ct 2) with slight wrist action as if throwing a frisbee.

Walk-Around Turn—Follower

Step	Foot & Direction	Degree & Direction of Turn	Rhythm	Musical Count	Comments
Steps 1–12 crossover					
13	RF sd		S	1–2	
14	LF fwd	1/2 R	Q	3	About face on
15	RF sip	1/2 R	Q	4	steps 14 & 15 turn first, then step
16	LF sd	1/4 R	S	5–6	
17	RF cl to LF		Q	7	
18	LF cl to RF		Q	8	

Note: See leader's note.

Open Break to Underarm Turn—Leader

Step	Foot & Direction	Degree & Direction of Turn	Rhythm	Musical Count	Comments
1	LF fwd		S	1–2	
2	RF sd		Q	3	
3	LF cl to RF		Q	4	
4	RF sd		S	5–6	
5	LF bwd		Q	7	
6	RF sip		Q	8	
7	LF sd		S	1–2	
8	RF cl to LF		Q	3	
9	LF sip		Q	4	
10	RF sd		S	5–6	
11	LF sip		Q	7	
12	RF cl to LF		Q	8	

Note: The man leads the open break on step 4 (ct 6) by opening with his R arm, bringing his L hip fwd, lowering his L arm. He leads the turn on step 7 (ct 1) by raising the arm above her head. A woman who turns well may want to do an extra 1 1/4 turns on step 10.

Open Break to Underarm Turn—Follower

Step	Foot & Direction	Degree & Direction of Turn	Rhythm	Musical Count	Comments
1	RF bwd		S	1–2	
2	LF sd		Q	3	
3	RF cl to LF		Q	4	
4	LF sd		S	5–6	
5	RF bwd		Q	7	
6	LF sip		Q	8	
7	RF sd		S	1–2	
8	LF fwd	1/4 R	Q	3	About face; on steps 8 & 9 turn first, then step
9	RF sip	1/2 R	Q	4	
10	LF sd	1/4 R	S	5–6	
11	RF sip		Q	7	
12	LF cl to RF		Q	8	

Note: On the turn use spotting to allow the body to move the foot. A woman who turns well may want to do an extra full turn on steps 10–12, making her turn 1 1/4 R.

Cross Body Lead—Leader

Step	Foot & Direction	Degree & Direction of Turn	Rhythm	Musical Count	Comments
1	LF fwd		S	1–2	
2	RF sd		Q	3	
3	LF cl to RF		Q	4	
4	RF bwd		S	5–6	
5	LF sd	1/4 L	Q	7	
6	RF cl to LF		Q	8	
7	LF fwd	1/4 L	S	1–2	Turn shoulders left
8	RF sd		Q	3	
9	LF cl to RF		Q	4	
10	RF bwd		S	5–6	
11	LF sd		Q	7	
12	RF cl to LF		Q	8	

Note: The man leads with his body; there is a slight inward rolling of the L hand and lowering of the left forearm on step 4 (ct 5) so that the knuckles are facing the partners; the man's toes and shoulders will find the new direction. He must not pull her or distort their dance frame.

Cross Body Lead—Follower

Step	Foot & Direction	Degree & Direction of Turn	Rhythm	Musical Count	Comments
1	RF bwd		S	1–2	
2	LF sd		Q	3	
3	RF cl to LF		Q	4	
4	LF fwd		S	5–6	Small step
5	RF fwd		Q	7	
6	LF fwd		Q	8	
7	RF bwd	1/2 L	S	1–2	
8	LF sd		Q	3	
9	RF cl to LF		Q	4	
10	LF fwd		S	5–6	
11	RF sd		Q	7	
12	LF cl to RF		Q	8	

Note: On step 4 (ct 5–6) the lady must wait until the man's L foot has cleared her path; her steps 4, 5, 6 move on a *very slight* diagonal away from her partner.

Peek-a-boo—Leader

Step	Foot & Direction	Degree & Direction of Turn	Rhythm	Musical Count	Comments
Steps 1–6 open break					
7	LF bwd	1/8 R	S	1–2	
8	RF fwd in CBMP		Q	3	5th fp
9	LF sip		Q	4	
10	RF sd	1/8 L	S	5–6	
11	LF bwd		Q	7	
12	RF sip		Q	8	
13–17	Repeat 7–12				
18–20	Repeat 7–9				
21	RF sd	1/8 L	S	5–6	
22	LF sip		Q	7	
23	RF cl to LF		Q	8	

Note: On step 7 (ct 1) the gentleman moves the lady to his R side leading her turn by giving a fingertip gesture of drawing his L hand toward his R shoulder. On step 8 (ct 3) he lowers his L hand slightly and touches her L shoulder with his R fingers. On step 10 (ct 5) he raises his L arm to lead her turn out of the peek-a-boo and back in front of him to the open break position. On step 21 (ct 5–6) he leads her into a turn to end the pattern and on step 22 (ct 7) he begins to move back into a closed Latin dance position.

Peek-a-boo

Peek-a-boo—Follower

Step	Foot & Direction	Degree & Direction of Turn	Rhythm	Musical Count	Comments
Steps 1–6 open break					
7	RF fwd	3/4 L	S	1–2	
8	LF sd		Q	3	5th fp
9	RF sip		Q	4	
10	LF fwd	3/4 R	S	5–6	Back in front of man to open break position
11	RF bwd		Q	7	
12	LF sip		Q	8	
13–17	Repeat 7–12				
18–20	Repeat 7–9				
21	LF fwd	3/4 R	S	5–6	
22	RF sip		Q	7	
23	LF cl to RF		Q	8	

Note: See leader's note. The woman usually takes her L arm out to the side in the open break lines; she may take her L arm high or across her body on steps 7–9, 13–14 and 18–20. She may do an extra turn on steps 22 and 23 resulting in 1 3/4 turns to come out of the pattern.

CHA-CHA

History

Cha-cha is a derivative of the Cuban mambo. It became enormously popular in the mid 1950's and is still enjoyed today.

Rhythm

Cha-cha is danced with three quick syncopated steps and 2 slow steps. The "1" count is the accented count and this is the held count where no foot step is taken. Cha-cha is faster than rumba, but slower than mambo. Dancers very often cue this: Q, SS, QQQ, SS or "1" break, step, cha-cha-cha, break, step.

Rhythm Time Signatures

Cha-cha is danced to music with 2/4 or 4/4 time.

Frames

The closed Latin dance frame (pp. 6 & 10) is used to give this dance its Latin look. Some patterns are danced in the open (p. 6) and sweetheart (p. 7) positions.

Technique

The correct technique is discussed in **Latin Dance** and **Rhythm Dance.** Cha-cha is more staccato than rumba. Due to the speed of the music, care must be taken not to develop sloppy, shuffling or lazy feet; each step must be precise, clean and small. Remember that the ''1'' count is accented with a hold.

Side to Side Basic—Leader

Step	Foot & Direction	Degree & Direction of Turn	Rhythm	Musical Count	Comments
1	LF sd		Q	1	
2	RF bwd		S	2	
3	LF sip		S	3	
4	RF sd		Q	4	
5	LF cl to RF		and	and	
6	RF sd		Q	1	
7	LF fwd		S	2	
8	RF sip		S	3	
9	LF sd		Q	4	
10	RF cl to LF		and	and	

Note: On steps 1 and 6 (ct 1) the 2nd part of the step has no foot movement but does have a hip change. There is syncopation of steps 4–6 and 9–1 with 3 quick steps taken in 2 beats of music.

Side to Side Basic—Follower

Step	Foot & Direction	Degree & Direction of Turn	Rhythm	Musical Count	Comments
1	RF sd		Q	1	
2	LF fwd		S	2	
3	RF sip		S	3	
4	LF sd		Q	4	
5	RF cl to LF		and	and	
6	LF sd		Q	1	
7	RF bwd		S	2	
8	LF sip		S	3	
9	RF sd		Q	4	
10	LF cl to RF		and	and	

Note: See leader's note. Some men will start this basic on step 2 (ct 2); still others will start at step 4 (ct 4) so the woman must be prepared to follow. Some people take the 3 "cha-cha-cha" steps, steps 4–6 and 9–1, in place rather than side, tog., side.

Progressive Basic—Leader

Step	Foot & Direction	Degree & Direction of Turn	Rhythm	Musical Count	Comments
1	LF sd		Q	1	
2	RF bwd		S	2	
3	LF sip		S	3	
4	RF fwd		Q	4	
5	LF fwd		and	and	
6	RF fwd		Q	1	
7	LF fwd		S	2	
8	RF sip		S	3	
9	LF bwd		Q	4	
10	RF bwd		and	and	
11	LF bwd		Q	1	
12	RF bwd		S	2	
13	LF sip		S	3	
14–23	Repeat 4–13				
24–28	Repeat 4–8				

Note: Some people dance all their patterns from this basic. Others use it as a dance pattern getting into and out of it from a side to side basic as illustrated above. The ending would be:

29	LF sd	Q	4
30	RF cl to LF	and	and
31–38	Steps 1–8 of side to side basic		

Progressive Basic—Follower

Step	Foot & Direction	Degree & Direction of Turn	Rhythm	Musical Count	Comments
1	RF sd		Q	1	
2	LF fwd		S	2	
3	RF sip		S	3	
4	LF bwd		Q	4	
5	RF bwd		and	and	
6	LF bwd		Q	1	
7	RF bwd		S	2	
8	LF sip		S	3	
9	RF fwd		Q	4	
10	LF fwd		and	and	
11	RF fwd		Q	1	
12	LF fwd		S	2	
13	RF sip		S	3	
14–23	Repeat 4–12				
24–28	Repeat 4–8				
29	RF sd		Q	4	
30	LF cl to RF		and	and	
31–38	Steps 1–8 of side to side basic				

Note: See leader's note.

Crossover—Leader

Step	Foot & Direction	Degree & Direction of Turn	Rhythm	Musical Count	Comments
Steps 1–6 of side to side basic					
7	LF fwd	1/4 R	S	2	Release heel of RF; pivot on ball
8	RF sip		S	3	
9	LF sd	1/4 L	Q	4	
10	RF cl to LF		and	and	
11	LF sd		Q	1	
12	RF fwd	1/4 L	S	2	Release heel of LF; pivot on ball
13	LF sip		S	3	
14–23	Repeat 4–13 with 1/4 turn R on step 4				
24	RF sd		Q	4	Take lady back into closed Latin dance frame
25	LF cl to RF		and	and	
26	RF sd		Q	1	
27	LF fwd		S	2	
28	RF sip		S	3	

Note: On step 4 (ct 4) the gentleman changes to a pistol hand hold (p. 10). On step 7 (ct 2) he draws the lady into a crossover. On steps 6 and 11 (ct 1) the couple are still facing one another joined by 2 hands. They should explode into the crossover. See rumba note (pp. 66–67) for details and for photo.

Crossover—Follower

Step	Foot & Direction	Degree & Direction of Turn	Rhythm	Musical Count	Comments
Steps 1–6 of side to side basic					
7	RF fwd	1/4 L	S	2	Release heel of LF; pivot on ball
8	LF sip		S	3	
9	RF sd	1/4 R	Q	4	
10	LF cl to RF		and	and	
11	RF sd		Q	1	
12	LF fwd	1/4 R	S	2	Release heel of RF; pivot on ball
13	RF sip		S	3	
14–23	Repeat 4–13 with 1/4 turn L on step 4				
24	LF sd		Q	4	
25	RF cl to LF		and	and	
26	LF sd		Q	1	
27	RF bwd		S	2	
28	LF sip		S	3	

Note: See leader's note.

Walk-Around Turn—Leader

Step	Foot & Direction	Degree & Direction of Turn	Rhythm	Musical Count	Comments
Steps 1–20 of crossover					
21	LF sd		Q	1	
22	RF fwd	1/4 L	S	2	About face;
23	LF sip	1/2 L	S	3	on steps 22 & 23 turn first,
24	RF sd	1/4 L	Q	4	then step
25	LF cl to RF		and	and	
26	RF sd		Q	1	
27	LF fwd		S	2	
28	RF sip		S	3	

Note: Use spotting on the turn making it snappy. Let the body move the foot. Lead with the L hand on step 21 (ct 1) with slight wrist action as if throwing a frisbee.

Walk-Around Turn—Follower

Step	Foot & Direction	Degree & Direction of Turn	Rhythm	Musical Count	Comments
Steps 1–20 of crossover					
21	RF sd		Q	1	
22	LF fwd	1/4 R	S	2	About face;
23	RF sip	1/2 R	S	3	on steps 22 & 23 turn first,
24	LF sd	1/4 R	Q	4	then step
25	RF cl to LF		and	and	
26	LF sd		Q	1	
27	RF bwd		S	2	
28	LF sip		S	3	

Note: See leader's note.

Open Break to Underarm Turn—Leader

Step	Foot & Direction	Degree & Direction of Turn	Rhythm	Musical Count	Comments
Steps 1–5 side to side basic					
6	RF sd		Q	1	
7	LF bwd		S	2	
8	RF sip		S	3	
9	LF sd		Q	4	
10	RF cl to LF		and	and	
11	LF sd		Q	1	
12	RF bwd		S	2	
13	LF sip		S	3	
14	RF sd		Q	4	
15	LF cl to RF		and	and	
16	RF sd		Q	1	
17	LF fwd		S	2	
18	RF sip		S	3	

Note: The man leads the open break on step 6 (ct 1) by opening with his R arm and by bringing his L hip fwd. He leads the turn on step 11 (ct 1) by raising the arm above her head. A woman who turns well may want to do an extra turn on steps 14–16.

Open Break to Underarm Turn—Follower

Step	Foot & Direction	Degree & Direction of Turn	Rhythm	Musical Count	Comments
Steps 1–5 side to side basic					
6	LF sd		Q	1	
7	RF bwd		S	2	
8	LF sip		S	3	
9	RF sd		Q	4	
10	LF cl to RF		and	and	
11	RF sd		Q	1	
12	LF fwd	1/4 R	S	2	About face;
13	RF sip	1/2 R	S	3	on steps 12 & 13 turn first,
14	LF sd	1/4 R	Q	4	then step
15	RF cl to LF		and	and	
16	LF sd		Q	1	
17	RF bwd		S	2	
18	LF sip		S	3	

Note: A woman who turns well may want to do an extra full turn on steps 14–16 making her turn 1 1/4 R.

Cross Body Lead—Leader

Step	Foot & Direction	Degree & Direction of Turn	Rhythm	Musical Count	Comments
Steps 1–7 of side to side basic					
8	RF sip	1/4 L	S	3	
9	LF sd		Q	4	
10	RF cl to LF		and	and	
11	LF sd		Q	1	
12	RF sip	1/4 L	S	2	
13	LF fwd		S	3	
14	RF sd		Q	4	
15	LF cl to RF		and	and	
16	RF sd		Q	1	
17	LF fwd		S	2	
18	RF sip		S	3	

Note: The man leads with his body; there is a slight inward rolling of the L hand and lowering of the left forearm on step 12 (ct 2) so that the knuckles are facing the partners; or he may use a pistol hand change (p. 10). The man's toes and shoulders will find the new direction. He must not pull his partner or distort their dance frame.

Cross Body Lead—Follower

Step	Foot & Direction	Degree & Direction of Turn	Rhythm	Musical Count	Comments
Steps 1–7 of side to side basic					
8	LF sip		S	3	
9	RF fwd		Q	4	
10	LF fwd		and	and	
11	RF fwd		Q	1	
12	LF fwd	1/2 L	S	2	
13	RF sip		S	3	
14	LF sd		Q	4	
15	RF cl to LF		and	and	
16	LF sd		Q	1	
17	RF bwd		S	2	
18	LF sip		S	3	

Note: On steps 9, 10, 11 the lady moves on a *very slight* diagonal away from her partner.

Peek-a-boo—Leader

Step	Foot & Direction	Degree & Direction on Turn	Rhythm	Musical Count	Comments
Steps 1–8 of open break					
9	LF fwd	⎤	Q	4	
10	RF cl to LF	⎬ 1/8 R	and	and	
11	LF sd	⎦	Q	1 ⎤	Small step
12	RF fwd in CBMP		S	2 ⎬	5th fp
13	LF sip		S	3	
14	RF sd	1/8 L	Q	4 ⎦	
15	LF cl to LF		and	and	
16	RF sd		Q	1	
17	LF bwd		S	2	
18	RF sip		S	3	
19–28	Repeat 9–18				
29–33	Repeat 9–13				
34	RF sd		Q	4	
35	LF cl to RF		and	and	
36	RF sd		Q	1	
37	LF fwd		S	2	
38	RF sip		S	3	

Note: On step 9 (ct 4) the man moves the woman to his R side leading her turn by giving a fingertip gesture of drawing his L hand toward his R shoulder. On step 11 (ct 1) he lowers his L hand slightly and touches her L shoulder with his R fingers. On step 14 (ct 4) he raises his L arm to lead her turn out of the peek-a-boo and back in front of him to the open break position. His R arm extends to his side. On step 34 he leads her into a turn to end the pattern and on step 37 he begins to move back into a closed Latin dance position. (See photo p. 71.)

Peek-a-boo—Follower

Step	Foot & Direction	Degree & Direction on Turn	Rhythm	Musical Count	Comments
Steps 1–8 of open break					
9	RF fwd	⌐	Q	4	
10	LF cl to RF	⌐ 3/4 L	and	and	
11	RF sd	_|	Q	1	
12	LF sd		S	2	⌐ 2nd fp
13	RF sip		S	3	_|
14	LF fwd	⌐	Q	4	
15	RF cl to LF	3/4 R	and	and	
16	LF sd	_|	Q	1	
17	RF bwd		S	2	
18	LF sip		S	3	
19–28	Repeat 9–18				
29–33	Repeat 9–13				
34	LF fwd	⌐	Q	4	
35	RF cl to LF	3/4 R	and	and	
36	LF sd	_|	Q	1	
37	RF bwd		S	2	
38	LF sip		S	3	

Note: See leader's note. The follower usually takes her L arm out to the side in the open break; she may take her L arm high or cross her body on steps 9–12, 19–21 and 29–30. She may do an extra turn on steps 34–36 resulting in 1 3/4 turns to finish the pattern.

MAMBO

History

Mambo originated in the sacred dances of voodoo ritual. In 1943 with *Mambo Jambo* the black Cuban band leader, Perez Prado, turned mambo into a dance sensation that swept the United States and became the dance craze of the 1950's. The movie, *Dirty Dancing,* repopularized mambo and introduced it to a new generation of dancers.

Rhythm

Mambo is the fastest of the three Cuban dances. The "one" count is the accented count; it is a held count and although there is a hip change, there is no foot step on this count.

Rhythm Time Signature

Frames

The closed Latin dance frame (p. 6), the open position (pp. 6–7) and the sweetheart position (p. 7) are used.

Technique

It is the speed of mambo which makes it difficult; the footwork must still be staccato and clean and the hips must continue to move with precision. Reread **Latin Dance** and **Rhythm Dance** for details on the proper technique.

Progressive or Passing Basic—Leader

Step	Foot & Direction	Degree & Direction of Turn	Rhythm	Musical Count	Comments
	Hold			1	
1	LF fwd		Q	2	
2	RF sip		Q	3	
3	LF sd & bwd		S	4–1	
4	RF bwd		Q	2	
5	LF sip		Q	3	
6	RF sd & fwd		S	4–1	

Note: The first count is held; if the leader has difficulty starting, he can touch his L foot in place on the "1" count to mark the downbeat. Some people progress steps 3 and 6 to 3rd foot positions; some progress them even further as in a cha-cha progressive basic. Some people dance a mambo basic where the feet come together on steps 3 and 6. Because of the speed all of the steps are small.

Progressive or Passing Basic—Follower

Step	Foot & Direction	Degree & Direction of Turn	Rhythm	Musical Count	Comments
	Hold			1	
1	RF bwd		Q	2	
2	LF sip		Q	3	
3	RF sd & fwd		S	4–1	
4	LF bwd		Q	2	
5	RF sip		Q	3	
6	LF sd & bwd		S	4–1	

Note: See leader's note.

Crossover—Leader

Step	Foot & Direction	Degree & Direction of Turn	Rhythm	Musical Count	Comments
Steps 1–5 of basic step					
6	RF sd		S	4–1	
7	LF fwd	1/4 R	Q	2	Release heel of RF; pivot on ball
8	RF sip		Q	3	
9	LF sd	1/4 L	S	4–1	
10	RF fwd	1/4 L	Q	2	Release heel of LF; pivot on ball
11	LF sip		Q	3	
12–17	Repeat steps 6–11 with 1/4 turn R on step 6				
18	RF sd	1/4 R	S	4–1	

Note: On step 6 (ct 4–1) the gentleman changes to a pistol hand hold (p. 10). On step 7 (ct 2) he draws the lady into a crossover. On step 18 he goes back to a closed dance position. See rumba note (pp. 66–67) for details and photo.

Crossover—Follower

Step	Foot & Direction	Degree & Direction of Turn	Rhythm	Musical Count	Comments
Steps 1–5 of basic step					
6	LF sd		S	4–1	
7	RF fwd	1/4 L	Q	2	Release heel of LF; pivot on ball
8	LF sip		Q	3	
9	RF sd	1/4 R	S	4–1	
10	LF fwd	1/4 R	Q	2	Release heel of RF; pivot on ball
11	RF sip		Q	3	
12–17	Repeat steps 6–11 with 1/4 turn L on step 6				
18	LF sd	1/4 R	S	4–1	

Note: See leader's note.

Walk-Around Turn—Leader

Step	Foot & Direction	Degree & Direction of Turn	Rhythm	Musical Count	Comments
Steps 1–14 of crossover					
15	LF sd	1/4 L	S	4–1	
16	RF fwd	1/4 L	Q	2	About face; on step 17 turn first then step
17	LF sip	1/2 L	Q	3	
18	RF sd	1/4 L	S	4–1	

Note: Use spotting on the turn making it sharp. Let the body move the foot. Lead with the L hand on step 15 (ct 1) as if throwing a frisbee.

Walk-Around Turn—Follower

Step	Foot & Direction	Degree & Direction of Turn	Rhythm	Musical Count	Comments
Steps 1–14 of crossover					
15	RF sd	1/4 R	S	4–1	
16	LF fwd	1/4 R	Q	2	About face; on step 17 turn first then step
17	RF sip	1/2 R	Q	3	
18	LF sd	1/4 R	S	4–1	

Note: See leader's note.

Open Break to Underarm Turn—Leader

Step	Foot & Direction	Degree & Direction of Turn	Rhythm	Musical Count	Comments
Steps 1–5 of basic step					
6	RF sd		S	4–1	
7	LF bwd		Q	2	
8	RF sip		Q	3	
9	LF sd		S	4–1	
10	RF bwd		Q	2	
11	LF sip		Q	3	
12	RF sd		S	4–1	

Note: The man leads the open break on step 6 (ct 1) by using a pistol hand change (p. 10), by opening with his R arm and by bringing his L hip fwd. He leads her turn on step 9 (ct 1) by raising the arm above her head if he wants her to turn to her R side or by making a "wall" with his L forearm if he wants her to turn in front of him. See follower's note.

Open Break to Underarm Turn—Follower

Step	Foot & Direction	Degree & Direction of Turn	Rhythm	Musical Count	Comments
Steps 1–5 of basic step					
6	LF sd		S	4–1	
7	RF bwd		Q	2	
8	LF sip		Q	3	
9	RF sd		S	4–1	
10	LF fwd	1/4 R	Q	2	About face; turn first, then step
11	RF fwd	1/2 R	Q	3	
12	LF sd	1/4 L	S	4–1	

Note: The man may make a "wall" with his L forearm on step 9; then she steps into him on step 10 changing her part to:

10	LF fwd		Q	2	About face; turn first then step
11	RF fwd	1/2 R	Q	3	
12	LF sd	1/2 R	S	4–1	

Crossbody Lead—Leader

Step	Foot & Direction	Degree & Direction of Turn	Rhythm	Musical Count	Comments
Steps 1–6 of basic step					
7	LF fwd		Q	2	
8	RF bwd	1/4 L	Q	3	
9	LF sd		S	4–1	
10	RF bwd	1/4 L	Q	2	
11	LF sip		Q	3	
12	RF sd		S	4–1	

Note: The man leads with his body by turning his shoulders and toe on step 8 (ct 3). He changes to a pistol hand hold on step 6 (ct 4–1) (p. 10). He may return to a basic or follow with a crossover beginning at step 7 of the crossover.

Crossbody Lead—Follower

Step	Foot & Direction	Degree & Direction of Turn	Rhythm	Musical Count	Comments
Steps 1–6 of basic step					
7	RF bwd		Q	2	
8	LF fwd		Q	3	
9	RF fwd		S	4–1	
10	LF fwd		Q	2	
11	RF bwd	1/2 L	Q	3	
12	LF sd		S	4–1	

Note: On steps 8 and 9 the woman moves on a *very slight* diagonal away from her partner.

Peek-a-boo—Leader

Step	Foot & Direction	Degree & Direction of Turn	Rhythm	Musical Count	Comments
Steps 1–8 of open break					
9	LF fwd	1/8 R	S	4–1	
10	RF fwd in CBMP		Q	2	⌉ 5th fp
11	LF sip		Q	3	⌋
12	RF sd	1/8 L	S	4–1	
13	LF bwd		Q	2	
14	RF sip		Q	3	
15–20	Repeat 9–14				
21–23	Repeat 9–11				
24	RF sd	1/8 L	S	4–1	
25	LF fwd		Q	2	
26	RF sip		Q	3	

Note: On step 9 (ct 4) the man moves the woman to his R side leading her turn by giving a fingertip gesture of drawing his L hand toward his R shoulder. On step 10 (ct 2) he lowers his L hand slightly and touches her L shoulder with his R fingers. On step 12 (ct 4) he raises his L arm to lead her turn out of the peek-a-boo and back in front of him to the open break position. On step 24 he leads her into a turn to end the pattern. On step 26 he moves back into a closed Latin dance position. (See photo p. 71.)

Peek-a-boo—Follower

Step	Foot & Direction	Degree & Direction of Turn	Rhythm	Musical Count	Comments
Steps 1–8 of open break					
9	RF fwd	3/4 L	S	4–1	
10	LF sd		Q	2	⌉ 2nd fp
11	RF sip		Q	3	⌋
12	LF fwd	3/4 R	S	4–1	
13	RF bwd		Q	2	
14	LF sip		Q	3	
15–20	Repeat 9–14				
21–23	Repeat 9–11				
24	LF fwd	3/4 R	S	4–1	
25	RF bwd		Q	2	
26	LF sip		Q	3	

Note: See leader's note. The follower usually takes her L arm out to the side in the open break; she may take her L arm high or across her body on steps 10, 16 and 22.

SAMBA

History

Samba, an old Brazilian style of dance with many variations, is African in origin. It has been performed as a street dance at carnival, the pre-Lenten celebration, for almost 100 years. It was introduced into the United States as a partner dance at the 1939 New York World's Fair. The American movie actress, Carmen Miranda, better known as the ''Brazilian bombshell,'' made samba a rage before World War II. The musical group ''Brazil 66'' and the bossa nova, a variation of the samba, helped to perpetuate interest in the dance. It was danced as samba hustle during the disco period.

Rhythm

There are 2 accented counts: the first is the ''Ah'' step which precedes the 1st and 3rd steps; the second accent is on counts 2 and 4 (on the 2nd beat of a 2/4 measure).

Rhythm Time Signature

Ah	1	&	2	Ah	3	&	4	Ah
Ah	Q	Q	S	Ah	Q	Q	S	Ah

Frame

The Latin dance frame is used (p. 6).

Technique

Samba, like waltz, has both rise and fall and sway which is perhaps why it is sometimes called the Brazilian waltz. Samba is, however, Latin and like other Latin dances it has a lot of hip action. The samba hip motion is totally unique. It originates with an ankle stretch and a forward thrusting of the thigh which in turn produces a pelvic tilt. This is followed by an up and down motion in the legs that is accompanied by a side to side or pinching motion in the ribs. At times the ankle stretching action is combined with a circular rotation of the hips as is seen, for example, in the com paso (or chasse) and volta patterns.

Basic Step—Leader

Step	Foot & Direction	Degree & Direction of Turn	Rhythm	Musical Count	Comments
	Stretch R ankle releasing R heel		Ah	Ah	Pelvic tilt
1	LF fwd		Q	1	LF brushes
2	RF fwd		Q	and	Wgt on ball
3	LF sip		S	2	of RF
	Stretch L ankle releasing L heel		Ah	Ah	Pelvic tilt
4	RF bwd		Q	3	RF brushes
5	LF bwd		Q	and	Wgt on ball
6	RF sip		S	4	of LF

Note: The ankle stretch and pelvic tilt push the thigh forward on the "Ah". On steps 1 and 3 the moving foot brushes the floor and, without losing contact, is lowered toe, ball, heel into the floor. On steps 2, 3, 5, and 6 the feet are in a 3rd fp; both knees are flexed and the motion is up and down into the floor while the ribs move from side to side. This is a ball change with 2 flexed knees. Cue the whole pattern: Toe (Ah) flat (1) toe (and) flat (2). This hip motion is used throughout samba.

Basic Step—Follower

Step	Foot & Direction	Degree & Direction of Turn	Rhythm	Musical Count	Comments
	Stretch L ankle releasing L heel		Ah	Ah	Pelvic tilt
1	RF bwd		Q	1	RF brushes
2	LF bwd		Q	and	Wgt on ball
3	RF sip		S	2	of LF
	Stretch R ankle releasing R heel		Ah	Ah	Pelvic tilt
4	LF fwd		Q	3	LF brushes
5	RF fwd		Q	and	Wgt on ball
6	LF sip		S	4	of RF

Note: See leader's note.

Left Box—Leader

Step	Foot & Direction	Degree & Direction of Turn	Rhythm	Musical Count	Comments
Stretch R ankle releasing R heel			Ah	Ah	Pelvic tilt
1	LF fwd		Q	1	
2	RF sd	1/4 L	Q	and	Wgt on ball of RF
3	LF cl to RF		S	2	
Stretch L ankle releasing L heel			Ah	Ah	Pelvic tilt
4	RF bwd		Q	3	
5	LF sd	1/4 L	Q	and	Wgt on ball of LF
6	RF cl to LF		S	4	
7–12	Repeat steps 1–6				

Note: On steps 1–3 sway L; on steps 4–6 sway R.

Left Box—Follower

Step	Foot & Direction	Degree & Direction of Turn	Rhythm	Musical Count	Comments
Stretch L ankle releasing L heel			Ah	Ah	Pelvic tilt
1	RF bwd		Q	1	
2	LF sd	1/4 L	Q	and	Wgt on ball of LF
3	RF cl to LF		S	2	
Stretch R ankle releasing R heel			Ah	Ah	Pelvic tilt
4	LF fwd		Q	3	
5	RF sd	1/4 L	Q	and	Wgt on ball of RF
6	LF cl to RF		S	4	
7–12	Repeat steps 1–6				

Note: On steps 1–3 sway R; on steps 4–6 sway L.

Forward and Back Com Paso—Leader

Step	Foot & Direction	Degree & Direction of Turn	Rhythm	Musical Count	Comments
Stretch R ankle releasing R heel			Ah	Ah	Pelvic tilt
1	LF fwd	1/4 L	Q	1	
2	RF sd		and	and	Ball of RF
3	LF cl to RF		Ah	Ah	Ball of LF
4	LF ip		Q	2	Settle down into both knees; flat of LF
5–10	Repeat 2–4 Twice				
Stretch L ankle releasing L heel			Ah	Ah	Pelvic tilt
11	RF bwd	1/4 L	Q	1	
12	LF sd		and	and	Ball of LF
13	RF cl to LF		Ah	Ah	Ball of RF
14	RF ip		Q	2	Settle down into both knees; flat of RF
15–20	Repeat 12–14 Twice				

Note: Some call this pattern a chasse. Sway to the L on the fwd step and to the R on the back step. Holding the sway and the circling of the hips forward, side, back and sides on steps 2–4 and 12–14 cue the lady.

Forward and Back Com Paso—Follower

Step	Foot & Direction	Degree & Direction of Turn	Rhythm	Musical Count	Comments
Stretch L ankle releasing L heel			Ah	Ah	Pelvic tilt
1	RF bwd	1/4 L	Q	1	
2	LF sd		and	and	Ball of LF
3	RF cl to LF		Ah	Ah	Ball of RF
4	RF ip		Q	2	Settle down into both knees; flat of RF
5–10	Repeat 2–4 Twice				
Stretch R ankle releasing R heel			Ah	Ah	Pelvic tilt
11	LF fwd	1/4 L	Q	1	
12	RF sd		and	and	Ball of RF
13	LF cl to RF		Ah	Ah	Ball of LF
14	LF ip		Q	2	Settle down into both knees; flat of LF
15–20	Repeat 12–14 Twice				

Note: See leader's note.

SWING

What's in a name? That which we call a rose by any other name would still smell as sweet. (Shakespeare)

It don't mean a thing if it ain't got that swing. (Duke Ellington)

Jive, jitterbug, lindy or swing, no matter what it's called, it has been and continues to be a favorite with dancers of all ages.

History

The Great Depression at the end of the 20's brought an end to the jazz age sound and heralded a new swing sound championed by the "King of Swing," Benny Goodman. This new percussive sound lead to new dances: the lindy hop, named after the national aeronautic hero, Charles Lindberg and the jitterbug. The jitterbug was revolutionary because of it athleticism (dancers were thrown up and around) and because of its solo parts, usually for the man. This dance endured through the 30's and 40's danced to big band swing, through the 50's danced to rock and roll and re-emerged in the 70's as a disco dance. Today it is danced to top 40's music and to country western music.

Rhythm

There are several different timings in swing: lindy timing, or 8 count swing; triple, double and single time in the 6 count swing and a 4 count swing. Generally, as the music becomes faster, steps are dropped off to help the dancer negotiate the faster tempo. Different generations and different dancers sometimes have preferred different timings; however, today, the triple time is probably the most commonly danced timing and is used competitively.

Rhythm Time Signatures

The 6 count triple, double, single time and west coast swings all use 1 1/2 measures of music; the 8 count or lindy uses 2 measures and the 4 count swing uses 1 measure. Many instructors cue the triple time rhythm: QQQ, QQQ, SS and cue the musical counts: 123, 123, rock step.

Triple time

Double time

Single time

Lindy

West Coast

4 count

Frames

In swing there is an open position which is face to face and hand to hand. He places his thumbs across her hooks (see pp. 6–7, 11). There is also a closed position where he uses the open hand hold with his left hand while maintaining a more traditional closed dance position with the rest of his body. (See pp. 6–7.)

Technique

This dance is a "spot" dance, one which does not move around the room. It calls for a relaxed appearance. Swing is danced with hip motion, quiet shoulders and soft knees. The weight is kept forward over the balls of the feet. The feet are placed, rather than shuffled, using the inside edge of the foot. The dancer should feel the floor pushing heavily into it.

This dance requires a lot of resistance; the couple's point of communication should be the hands not the elbows or shoulders. See hook exercise (p. 19).

Proper resistance with hand connection

Incorrect; connection at shoulders

The leader should control his partner's distance from him by keeping flex in his arms. Both partners must be wary of hyperextending the elbow or shoulder joints; the arms should be kept in front of the body so that the elbow never slips behind the body.

The image for this dance is a yoyo. The man stays in one spot on the floor while the woman travels. He sends his yoyo away and brings her back and when the couple become proficient, he even does tricks with his yoyo sending her around his body and through his legs! Because this is a fast dance most of the leads come a count before the desired move, generally on the "step" of the rock step. Caution must be used on the rock step to avoid a large back step or a backwards shift of weight. The feet should overlap slightly in a toe to heel 5th foot position (p. 8).

In the mid 1930's Dean Collins brought the lindy as it was danced at Harlem's Savoy Ballroom to California. What developed in the west was a linear or slot dance versus the more rounded swing. This California version was called the western swing until the late 1950's when the name was changed to west coast swing. It is typically danced to slower music than the jive or jitterbug and consequently a lot of popular rhythm and blues as well as country-western music lends itself to this dance. A prep step is included as a bridge for those students who want to combine west coast and traditional swing patterns in the same piece of music.

Basic Pattern—Triple Time—Leader

Step	Foot & Direction	Degree & Direction of Turn	Rhythm	Musical Count	Comments
1	LF sd		Q	1	Short step
2	RF cl to LF		and	and	Short step
3	LF sd		Q	2	Accented count; *slightly* longer step
4	RF sip		Q	3	Short step
5	LF cl to RF		and	and	Short step
6	RF sd		Q	4	*Slightly* longer step
7	LF bwd		S	5	Keep wgt fwd over ball of foot
8	RF sip		S	6	

Basic Pattern—Triple Time—Follower

Step	Foot & Direction	Degree & Direction of Turn	Rhythm	Musical Count	Comments
1	RF sd		Q	1	Short step
2	LF cl to RF		and	and	Short step
3	RF sd		Q	2	Accented count; *slightly* longer step
4	LF sip		Q	3	Short step
5	RF cl to LF		and	and	Short step
6	LF sd		Q	4	*Slightly* longer step
7	RF bwd		S	5	Keep wgt fwd over ball of foot
8	LF sip		S	6	

Note: The accent is on the "2" and "4" counts; the basic is syncopated with 3 steps taken to two beats of music. The woman and man both step back on step 7. Many instructors cue the rhythm: QQQ, QQQ, SS, and cue the musical counts: 123, 123, rock step. In closed position both partners hinge open (1/8) like a door opening slightly on steps 7 and 8.

Basic Pattern—Double Time—Leader

Step	Foot & Direction	Degree & Direction of Turn	Rhythm	Musical Count	Comments
1	LF tch		Q	1	Use toe or ball of foot to "dig"
2	LF sip		Q	2	Use flat of foot to "step"
3	RF tch		Q	3	
4	RF sip		Q	4	
5	LF bwd		Q	5	
6	RF sip		Q	6	

Note: Variations: place step 1 near R foot and step 2 sd, step 3 near L foot and step 4 sd; use the heel on steps 1 and 3 instead of the toe.

Basic Pattern—Double Time—Follower

Step	Foot & Direction	Degree & Direction of Turn	Rhythm	Musical Count	Comments
1	RF tch		Q	1	Use toe or ball of foot to "dig"
2	RF sip		Q	2	Use flat of foot to "step"
3	LF tch		Q	3	
4	LF sip		Q	4	
5	RF bwd		Q	5	
6	LF sip		Q	6	

Note: Variations: Place step 1 near L foot and step 2 sd, step 3 near R foot and step 4 sd; use heel on steps 1 and 3 instead of the toe.

Basic Pattern—Single Time—Leader

Step	Foot & Direction	Degree & Direction of Turn	Rhythm	Musical Count	Comments
1	LF sip		S	1–2	
2	RF sip		S	3–4	
3	LF bwd		Q	5	
4	RF sip		Q	6	

Note: This pattern can be danced in 4 counts using all Q steps.

Basic Pattern—Single Time—Follower

Step	Foot & Direction	Degree & Direction of Turn	Rhythm	Musical Count	Comments
1	RF sip		S	1–2	
2	LF sip		S	3–4	
3	RF bwd		Q	5	
4	LF sip		Q	6	

Turning Basic—Leader or Follower
Single, Double, or Triple Time

This basic is usually turned from a closed dance position to the right or clockwise on steps 1–6 (counts 1–4). The man should lead the rotation with the left side of his body bringing his left side in front of his partner.

Underarm Turn Right—Leader

Step	Foot & Direction	Degree & Direction of Turn	Rhythm	Musical Count	Comments
1	LF sd		Q	1	Short step
2	RF cl to LF		and	and	Release L
3	LF sd		Q	2	heel; turn on
4	LF ip pivot	1/4 L	and	and	ball of foot
5	RF sd		Q	3	
6	LF cl to RF		and	and	
7	RF sd		Q	4	
8	LF bwd		S	5	
9	RF sip		S	6	

Note: Some people call this an arch turn because the woman turns under an arch made by her R arm and the man's L arm. The man leads on step 8 (count 6) of preceding pattern; from cp man raises L arm and gives her a gentle push with his R hand on her back; from op man raises his L arm and gives a fingertip flick with his R hand. During the turn the man holds the lady's arm right above her head; holding it higher will pull her off balance. He should allow her fingers to turn within his.

Underarm Turn Right—Follower

Step	Foot & Direction	Degree & Direction of Turn	Rhythm	Musical Count	Comments
1	RF fwd		Q	1	Basic arm
2	LF fwd	3/4 R	and	and	style; bring L
3	RF fwd		Q	2	arm in
4	RF ip pivot		and	and	
5	LF sd		Q	3	Take left arm
6	RF cl to LF		and	and	out to the side (p. 12)
7	LF sd		Q	4	
8	RF bwd		S	5	
9	LF sip		S	6	

Note: Other arm styling is possible (pp. 12–14). The woman must keep the R elbow under the R wrist as she turns.

Underarm Turn Left—Leader

Step	Foot & Direction	Degree & Direction of Turn	Rhythm	Musical Count	Comments
1	LF sd		Q	1	
2	RF cl to LF		and	and	
3	LF sd		Q	2	
4	LF ip pivot	1/2 R	and	and	Release L heel; turn on ball of foot
5	RF sd		Q	3	
6	LF cl to RF		and	and	
7	RF sd		Q	4	
8	LF bwd		S	5	
9	RF sip		S	6	

Note: Some people call this a loop turn. The man leads on step 8 (count 6) of preceding pattern, usually from an open position which is safer and more attractive. The man must first move the woman by giving a fingertip gesture of drawing his L hand toward his R shoulder; after he has moved his partner, he turns. Again he must keep his hand close to her head as she turns so she won't by pulled off balance. Her fingers turn within his. This is often led after the Underarm Turn Right.

Underarm Turn Left—Follower

Step	Foot & Direction	Degree & Direction of Turn	Rhythm	Musical Count	Comments
1	RF fwd		Q	1	Basic arm style; bring L arm in
2	LF fwd		and	and	
3	RF fwd		Q	2	
4	RF ip pivot	1/2 L	and	and	Release R heel; turn on ball of foot
5	LF sd		Q	3	Take L arm out to the side (p. 12)
6	RF cl to LF		and	and	
7	LF sd		Q	4	
8	RF bwd		S	5	
9	LF sip		S	6	

Note: Other arm styling is possible on all of these patterns. (See pp. 12–14.)

Backpass A—Leader

Step	Foot & Direction	Degree & Direction of Turn	Rhythm	Musical Count	Comments
1	LF sd		Q	1	
2	RF cl to LF		and	and	
3	LF sd		Q	2	
4	LF ip pivot	1/2 L	and	and	Release L heel; turn on ball of foot; turn into her R arm
5	RF sd		Q	3	
6	LF cl to RF		and	and	
7	RF sd		Q	4	
8	LF bwd		S	5	
9	RF sip		S	6	

Note: The man leads on step 8 (count 6) of preceding pattern from an open position. The man must first move her by giving a fingertip gesture of drawing his L hand toward his L hip; he must keep his R forearm slightly above his waist so he doesn't get trapped. Before he turns, he places her R hand on the R side of his waist so she can trace his waist as he turns; as she slides off the L side of his waist, he retrieves her R hand to R hand in handshake position.

Backpass A—Follower

Step	Foot & Direction	Degree & Direction of Turn	Rhythm	Musical Count	Comments
1	RF fwd		Q	1	Basic arm style; bring L arm in
2	LF fwd		and	and	
3	RF fwd		Q	2	
4	RF ip pivot	1/2 R	and	and	Release R heel; turn on ball of foot;
5	LF sd		Q	3	Take L arm out to side
6	RF cl to LF		and	and	
7	LF sd		Q	4	
8	RF bwd		S	5	
9	LF sip		S	6	

Note: The woman traces the man's waist with her R fingers while he turns.

Backpass B—Leader

Step	Foot & Direction	Degree & Direction of Turn	Rhythm	Musical Count	Comments
1	LF sd		Q	1	
2	RF cl to LF		and	and	
3	LF sd		Q	2	
4	LF ip pivot	1/2 L	and	and	Release L heel; turn on ball of foot & switch hands
5	RF sd		Q	3	
6	LF cl to RF		and	and	
7	RF sd		Q	4	
8	LF bwd		S	5	
9	RF sip		S	6	

Note: The man leads on step 8 (count 6) of preceding pattern from a handshake R hand to R hand position. The man must first move the woman by drawing her along his R side. As he turns he passes her R hand from his R hand to his L hand behind his back.

Backpass B—Follower

Step	Foot & Direction	Degree & Direction of Turn	Rhythm	Musical Count	Comments
1	RF fwd		Q	1	Basic arm style; bring L arm in
2	LF fwd		and	and	
3	RF fwd		Q	2	
4	RF ip pivot	1/2 R	and	and	Release R heel; turn on ball of foot;
5	LF sd		Q	3	Take L arm out to side
6	RF cl to LF		and	and	
7	LF sd		Q	4	
8	RF bwd		S	5	
9	LF sip		S	6	

Sugarpush—Leader

Step	Foot & Direction	Degree & Direction of Turn	Rhythm	Musical Count	Comments
1	LF fwd		Q	1	OP
2	RF cl to LF		and	and	ROP
3	LF sip		Q	2	ROP
4	LF ip pivot	1/2 R	and	and	Release L heel; turn on ball of foot to LOP
5	RF sip		Q	3	LOP
6	LF sip		and	and	LOP
7	RF sip		Q	4	LOP
8	LF bwd		S	5	OP
9	RF sip		S	6	OP

Note: The man leads a double hand hold (p. 11) on step 4 (count 3) of the preceding basic. Couples should be ROP and LOP (p. 5) with half of each body overlapping the other; they should not be hip to hip. No more than three of these would be danced in a row followed by an underarm turn left to get out of the pattern.

Sugarpush—Follower

Step	Foot & Direction	Degree & Direction of Turn	Rhythm	Musical Count	Comments
1	RF fwd		Q	1	OP
2	LF cl to RF		and	and	ROP
3	RF sip		Q	2	ROP
4	RF ip pivot	1/2 R	and	and	Release R heel; turn on ball of foot to LOP
5	LF sip		Q	3	LOP
6	RF sip		and	and	LOP
7	LF sip		Q	4	LOP
8	RF bwd		S	5	OP
9	LF sip		S	6	OP

Throwout—Leader

Step	Foot & Direction	Degree & Direction of Turn	Rhythm	Musical Count	Comments
Steps 1–8 of basic pattern					
9	LF fwd		Q	1	short steps
10	RF fwd	1/4 L	and	and	passing feet
11	LF fwd		Q	2	
12			and	and	Release R hand
13	RF sd		Q	3	
14	LF cl to RF		and	and	
15	RF sd		Q	4	
16	LF bwd		S	5	
17	RF sip		S	6	5th fp

Note: The man leads the lady past him into an open swing position on steps 9–11, using his body and momentum to carry her away.

Throwout—Follower

Step	Foot & Direction	Degree & Direction of Turn	Rhythm	Musical Count	Comments
Steps 1–8 of basic pattern					
9	RF fwd	1/8 R	Q	1	
10	LF fwd		and	and	
11	RF fwd		Q	2	
12	RF pivots	1/8 L	and	and	
13	LF sd		Q	3	
14	RF cl to LF		and	and	
15	LF sd		Q	4	
16	RF bwd		S	5	
17	LF sip		S	6	5th fp

Note: Wait for the man to release you. Follow his directional lead steps 12–15; he may lead you to face him or lead you to his side. The woman may choose to do a kick ball change on the last steps changing her part to:

16	RF kick		Q	5	Kick
17	RF bwd		and	and	ball change
18	LF sip		Q	6	

Lindy Basic—Leader

Step	Foot & Direction	Degree & Direction of Turn	Rhythm	Musical Count	Comments
1	LF sd		Q	1	
2	RF cl to LF		and	and	
3	LF sd		Q	2	
4	RF sip		S	3	
5	LF sip		S	4	
6	RF sd		Q	5	
7	LF cl to RF		and	and	
8	RF sd		Q	6	
9	LF bwd		S	7	
10	RF sip		S	8	

Note: This basic can be turned to the right.

Lindy Basic—Follower

Step	Foot & Direction	Degree & Direction of Turn	Rhythm	Musical Count	Comments
1	RF sd		Q	1	
2	LF cl to RF		and	and	
3	RF sd		Q	2	
4	LF sip		S	3	
5	RF sip		S	4	
6	LF sd		Q	5	
7	RF cl to LF		and	and	
8	LF sd		Q	6	
9	RF bwd		S	7	
10	LF sip		S	8	

Lindy Side to Side—Leader

Step	Foot & Direction	Degree & Direction of Turn	Rhythm	Musical Count	Comments
Throwout					
1	LF sip		Q	1	
2	RF sip		and	and	
3	LF sip		Q	2	
4	RF bwd	3/4 R	S	3 ⌐	His steps are very small; he is like the center of a wheel
5	LF bwd		S	4	
6	RF bwd		S	5	
7	LF bwd		S	6 ⌐	
8	RF sd		Q	1	
9	LF cl to RF		and	and	
10	RF sip		Q	2	
11	LF bwd		S	3	
12	RF sip		S	4	
13	LF sd	1/8 R	Q	1	
14	RF cl to LF		and	and	
15	LF sip		Q	2	
16	RF sip		Q	3	
17	LF sip		and	and	
18	RF sip		Q	4	
19	LF bwd		S	5	
20	RF sip		S	6	

Note: The man moves the woman to his L side by drawing his L hand toward his L hip on step 12 of the throwout. He then slides his L hand and her R hand behind his back, leaving her R hand there and moving his L hand behind her back. They walk around together on steps 4–7 (counts 3–6). He walks bwd; she walks fwd. On steps 8–9 (counts 1 and 2) he passes her in front of him from his L side to his R side. He then uses his R hand on the back of her shoulder and his L hand to the front of her L hip to lead her into a tuck-in turn on step 12 (count 4). He turns her in on steps 13–15 (counts 1 and 2), then turns her out on steps 16–18 (counts 3 and 4).

Lindy Side to Side—Follower

Step	Foot & Direction	Degree & Direction of Turn	Rhythm	Musical Count	Comments
Throwout					
1	RF sd		Q	1	
2	LF cl to RF		and	and	
3	RF sd		Q	2	
4	LF fwd		S	3	Lady styles
5	RF fwd		S	4	L arm
6	LF fwd		S	5	
7	RF fwd		S	6	
8	LF fwd	1/4 R	Q	1	
9	RF fwd	1/4 R	and	and	
10	LF fwd	1/2 R	Q	2	Release L heel & pivot on ball of L foot
11	RF bwd		S	3	
12	LF sip		S	4	
13	RF fwd	1/8 L	Q	1	Lady brings arms in,
14	LF sip		and	and	crossing her chest, keeping her elbows down
15	RF sip		Q	2	
16	LF fwd		Q	3	Lady raises arms over head keeping elbows down & into her own body until she's cleared her partner
17	RF fwd	full R	and	and	
18	LF fwd		Q	4	
19	RF bwd		S	5	
20	LF sip		S	6	

Note: See leader's note. The woman can do 2 full turns on steps 16–18 (counts 3 and 4).

Prep Step—Leader

Step	Foot & Direction	Degree & Direction of Turn	Rhythm	Musical Count	Comments
1	LF sd		Q	1	Short step
2	RF cl to LF		and	and	Short step
3	LF sd		Q	2	
4	RF sip		Q	3	
5	LF cl to RF		and	and	Short step
6	RF sd		Q	4	
7	LF sd		S	5	Checking action; side or 2nd position break
8	RF sip		S	6	
9	LF cl to RF	1/4 L	Q	7	
10	RF sip		and	and	
11	LF sip		Q	8	Release partner

Note: Steps 1–8 are danced in a closed position. The follower is thrown out on steps 9–10 and the pattern ends in open position. See *Note* p. 111.

Prep Step—Follower

Step	Foot & Direction	Degree & Direction of Turn	Rhythm	Musical Count	Comments
1	RF sd		Q	1	Short step
2	LF cl to RF		and	˙and	Short step
3	RF sd		Q	2	
4	LF sip		Q	3	
5	RF cl to LF		and	and	Short step
6	LF sd		Q	4	
7	RF bwd		S	5	5th position break
8	LF sip		S	6	
9	RF fwd	1/8 R	Q	7	
10	LF fwd		and	and	
11	RF fwd	3/8 L	Q	8	

Sugar Push—Leader

Step	Foot & Direction	Degree & Direction of Turn	Rhythm	Musical Count	Comments
1	LF bwd		S	1	
2	RF bwd		S	2	
3	LF cl to RF		Q	3	
4	RF sip		Q	and	
5	LF fwd		Q	4	
6	RF to LF		Q	5	5th foot position RF back
7	LF sip		Q	and	
8	RF sip		Q	6	

Note: Variation: on step 3 the LF touches closing to the RF and step 4 is eliminated.

Sugar Push—Follower

Step	Foot & Direction	Degree & Direction of Turn	Rhythm	Musical Count	Comments
1	RF fwd		S	1	
2	LF fwd		S	2	
3	RF cl to LF		Q	3	
4	LF sip		Q	and	
5	LF bwd		Q	4	
6	LF to RF		Q	5	5th foot position LF back
7	RF sip		Q	and	
8	LF sip		Q	6	

Note: Variation: on step 3 the RF touches closing to the LF and step 4 is eliminated.

Underarm Turn Left—Leader

Step	Foot & Direction	Degree & Direction of Turn	Rhythm	Musical Count	Comments
1	LF bwd		S	1	
2	RF sip		S	2	
3	LF fwd	1/2 R	Q	3	About face
4	RF sip		and	and	
5	LF fwd		Q	4	
6	RF to LF		Q	5	5th fp
7	LF sip		and	and	
8	RF sip		Q	6	

Note: Leader lowers L hand to lead Lady's turn on step 4 (and).

Underarm Turn Left—Follower

Step	Foot & Direction	Degree & Direction of Turn	Rhythm	Musical Count	Comments
1	RF fwd		S	1	
2	LF fwd		S	2	
3	RF fwd	1/2 L	Q	3	LF xif
4	LF bwd		and	and	
5	RF bwd		Q	4	
6	LF to RF		Q	5	5th fp
7	RF sip		and	and	
8	LF sip		Q	6	

Right Side Pass & Inside Turn—Leader

Step	Foot & Direction	Degree & Direction of Turn	Rhythm	Musical Count	Comments
1	LF sd	1/4 L	S	1	⌐ lead lady
2	RF sip		S	2	⌐ past
3	LF cl to RF	1/4 L	Q	3	lead UAT L
4	RF sip		and	and	
5	LF fwd		Q	4	
6	RF bwd		Q	5	5th fp
7	LF sip		and	and	
8	RF sip		Q	6	

Note: This pattern begins R hand to R hand. The hand change can be made on step 8 of the underarm turn left. On step 5 (count 4) the man can loop his R hand over his own head, then release with his R so she can slide her R hand down his L arm on steps 6–8.

Right Side Pass & Inside Turn—Follower

Step	Foot & Direction	Degree & Direction of Turn	Rhythm	Musical Count	Comments
1	RF fwd		S	1	
2	LF fwd		S	2	
3	RF fwd	1/2 L	Q	3	⌐ small steps,
4	LF fwd	1/2 L	and	and	feet under
5	RF bwd	1/2 L	Q	4	⌐ body
6	LF bwd		Q	5	5th fp
7	RF sip		and	and	
8	LF sip		Q	6	

Note: This pattern begins R hand to R hand. The hand change can be made on step 8 of the underarm turn left. On step 5 (count 4) the man can loop his R hand over his own head, then release with his R so she can slide her R hand down his L arm on steps 6–8.

Whip to Outside Turn—Leader

Step	Foot & Direction	Degree & Direction of Turn	Rhythm	Musical Count	Comments
1	LF bwd		S	1	
2	RF sip		S	2	cp
3	LF fwd	1/2 R	Q	3	
4	RF sip		and	and	
5	LF sd		Q	4	
6	RF xib		S	5	
7	LF sd	1/4 R	S	6	
8	RF bwd	1/4 R	Q	7	5th fp
9	LF sip		and	and	
10	RF sip		Q	8	

Note: Man takes lady into closed dance position on step 2 and leads UAT R on step 7.

Whip to Outside Turn—Follower

Step	Foot & Direction	Degree & Direction of Turn	Rhythm	Musical Count	Comments
1	RF fwd		S	1	
2	LF fwd		S	2	
3	RF bwd	1/2 R	Q	3	
4	LF cl to RF		and	and	
5	RF fwd		Q	4	
6	LF bwd	1/2 R	S	5	
7	RF fwd	1/2 R	S	6	
8	LF bwd	1/2 R	Q	7	
9	RF fwd		and	and	5th fp
10	LF sip		Q	8	

Note: On step 5 lady steps between man's feet. She may do 2 1/2 turns on steps 6–10.

POLKA

The Parisians have "never imported anything more ridiculous or ungraceful than this polka. It is a hybrid confusion of Scotch Lilt, Irish Jig and Bohemian Waltz, and needs only to be seen once to be avoided for ever." *The Illustrated London News* April, 1844

History

Luckily the view expressed by *The Illustrated London News* was a minority view. The polka which originated in Bohemia (Czechoslovakia) spread like wildfire to France where polka mania ensued. From France it traveled to England and then to America; it endures today as one of the most widely danced ballroom dances.

Rhythm

The accent falls on the downbeat or first beat of each measure. While some dancers begin polka with a hop on the upbeat, it is easier to start on the accented first count.

Rhythm Time Signature

Frame

The closed position dance frame is most common (pp. 2–3). Jesse polka is danced in a sweetheart or varsouvienne position (p. 7).

Styling

There are almost as many varieties of polka as there are polka dancers. Some hop throughout the dance; some hop only on the upbeat;
some dance smoothly as if dancing waltz. Country-western styling
uses a clogging like brush on the upbeat. Still others lift the knee out
to the side as they hop. Any of these stylings can be attractive. The
key seems to be to control the size of the steps, keeping them small,
and to harness the exuberance which the dance generates.

Forward Basic—Leader

Step	Foot & Direction	Degree & Direction of Turn	Rhythm	Musical Count	Comments
1	LF fwd		Q	1	Flat
2	RF cl to LF		Q	2	Ball
3	LF fwd		S ⌉	3	Flat-short step
4	LF ip		⌋	4	Hop or other styling
5	RF fwd		Q	1	Flat
6	LF cl to RF		Q	2	Ball
7	RF fwd		S ⌉	3	Flat-short step
8	RF ip		⌋	4	Hop or other styling

Note: An underarm turn right may be led by the man on step 1 by raising his L arm.

Forward Basic—Follower

Step	Foot & Direction	Degree & Direction of Turn	Rhythm	Musical Count	Comments
1	RF bwd		Q	1	Flat
2	LF cl to RF		Q	2	Ball
3	RF bwd		S ⌉	3	Flat-short step
4	RF ip		⌋	4	Hop or other styling
5	LF bwd		Q	1	Flat
6	RF cl to LF		Q	2	Ball
7	LF bwd		S ⌉	3	Flat-short step
8	LF ip		⌋	4	Hop or other styling

Right Turning Basic—Leader

Step	Foot & Direction	Degree & Direction of Turn	Rhythm	Musical Count	Comments
1	LF sd	⎤	Q	1	Flat
2	RF cl to LF	1/4 R	Q	2	Ball
3	LF sip	⎦	S ⎤	3	Flat
4	LF ip		⎦	4	Hop or other styling
5	RF sd	⎤	Q	1	Flat
6	LF cl to RF	1/4 R	Q	2	Ball
7	RF sip	⎦	S ⎤	3	Flat
8	RF ip		⎦	4	Hop or other styling
9–16	Repeat 1–8				

Note: Alternate 4 forward basics with 1 full right turning basic, back to the 4 forward basics, 1 full right turning basic etc. . . . to create an attractive pattern and eliminate the dizziness which beginners often experience with continuous turning. More experienced dancers will want to turn steps 1–3 and 5–6 1/2 instead of 1/4 and then they will alternate 2 forward basics with 1 full right turning basic. To turn 1/2, the person stepping with the LF takes large steps to get around the person stepping with the RF. The person stepping with the RF takes small steps and rotates his shoulders strongly to help pull his partner around him. In effect, the partners alternate being pivots for one another. They must keep their hips facing one another throughout. There is sway on a turning polka basic just as there is sway in samba or waltz. The dancer sways and turns his head to the L as he steps with the L and to the R as he steps with the R. This basic can also be turned left.

Right Turning Basic—Follower

Step	Foot & Direction	Degree & Direction of Turn	Rhythm	Musical Count	Comments
1	RF sd		Q	1	Flat
2	LF cl to RF	1/4 R	Q	2	Ball
3	RF sip		S	3	Flat
4	RF ip			4	Hop or other styling
5	LF sd		Q	1	Flat
6	RF cl to RF	1/4 R	Q	2	Ball
7	LF sip		S	3	Flat
8	LF ip			4	Hop or other styling

Note: See leader's note.

Promenade—Leader

Step	Foot & Direction	Degree & Direction of Turn	Rhythm	Musical Count	Comments
1	LF fwd		Q	1	Flat
2	RF cl to LF		Q	2	Ball
3	LF fwd		S	3	Flat-short step
4	LF ip			4	Hop or other styling
5	RF fwd		Q	1	Flat
6	LF cl to RF		Q	2	Ball
7	RF fwd		S	3	Flat-short step
8	RF ip			4	Hop or other styling

Note: This promenade position has the partners side by side. They can maintain closed dance frame hold or switch to a behind the back hold with the spare hands (gentleman's L; lady's R) held out to the sides or on the hips. The leader usually enters this pattern with a turning basic releasing the lady at the end and allowing momentum to carry her to his side. To end this pattern the man turns R pivoting on the ball of his RF to face the woman and proceeds with his LF to lead his next pattern. Polka, like waltz, is a fine dance to dance with young children. Use the varsouvienne position (p. 7); make sure your little partner can skip and away you go, skipping down LOD. You can turn on the corners of the dance floor; turn L with the adult acting as the pivot taking steps in place and turning his body as the child skips around the outside. This polka comes naturally to children and requires no sideline dance instruction. It is ideally suited to weddings and dance situations with polka bands. If you have the time, teach your little friend a polka step as it is danced in promenade, but with both of you beginning with the L foot so your partner can copy your footwork. Use the cue words "bumble bee" or "polka step." Add the hop once your partner has mastered the fwd; close, fwd footwork.

Promenade—Leader

Step	Foot & Direction	Degree & Direction of Turn	Rhythm	Musical Count	Comments
1	RF fwd		Q	1	Flat
2	LF cl to RF		Q	2	Ball
3	RF fwd		S	3	Flat-short step
4	RF ip			4	Hop or other styling
5	LF fwd		Q	1	Flat
6	RF cl to LF		Q	2	Ball
7	LF fwd		S	3	Flat-short step
8	LF ip			4	Hop or other styling

Note: See leader's note.

Right turning basic

Promenade

Turning Passes—Leader

Step	Foot & Direction	Degree & Direction of Turn	Rhythm	Musical Count	Comments
Steps 1–8 Promenade					
9	LF fwd	1/4 R	Q	1	across partner
10	RF fwd	1/8 R	Q	2	small step
11	LF fwd	1/8 R	S ⌉	3	small step
12	LF ip		⌡	4	optional hop
13	RF fwd	1/4 R	Q	1 ⌉	turning 1/2 R
14	LF fwd	1/4 R	Q	2 ⌡	
15	RF sip		S ⌉	3	
16	RF IP		⌡	4	optional hop
17–24 Steps 1–8 Promenade					
25	LF sip		Q	1	lead lady
26	RF sip		Q	2	
27	LF sip		S ⌉	3	
28	LF ip		⌡	4	optional hop
29	RF sip		Q	1	
30	LF sip		Q	2	
31	RF sip		S ⌉	3	R hand behind lady
32	RF ip		⌡	4	optional hop

Turning Passes—Follower

Step	Foot & Direction	Degree & Direction of Turn	Rhythm	Musical Count	Comments
Steps 1–8 Promenade					
9	RF sip		Q	1	
10	LF sip		Q	2	
11	RF sip		S ⌉	3	
12	RF ip		⌡	4	optional hop
13	LF sip		Q	1	
14	RF sip		Q	2	
15	LF sip		S ⌉	3	
16	LF ip		⌡	4	optional hop
17–24 Steps 1–8 Promenade					
25	RF fwd	1/4 R	Q	1	across partner
26	LF fwd	1/8 R	Q	2	small step
27	RF fwd	1/8 R	S ⌉	3	small step
28	RF ip		⌡	4	
29	LF fwd	1/4 R	Q	1	turning 1/2 R
30	RF fwd	1/4 R	Q	2	
31	LF sip		S ⌉	3	
32	LF ip		⌡	4	

Jesse Polka—Leader and Follower

Many people enjoy this form of polka; it is an excellent way to make the polka less strenuous. Assume varsouvienne position (p. 7). Both parners begin with the L foot.

Step	Foot & Direction	Degree & Direction of Turn	Rhythm	Musical Count	Comments
Facing LOD					
1	LF fwd		Q	1	Flat
2	RF cl to LF		Q	2	Ball
3	LF fwd		S ⌐	3	Flat-short step
4	LF ip		⌐	4	Hop or other styling
5	RF fwd		Q	1	Flat
6	LF cl to RF		Q	2	Ball
7	RF fwd		S ⌐	3	Flat-short step
8	RF ip		⌐	4	Hop or other styling
9–16	Repeat 1–8				
17	L heel fwd		Q	1	
18	LF cl to RF		Q	2	
19	R toe bwd		S ⌐	3	
20	R toe tch to LF		⌐	4	
21	R heel fwd		Q	1	
22	RF cl to LF		Q	2	
23	L heel fwd		S ⌐	3	
24	LF xif over RF		⌐	4	

Repeat from beginning; those who are creative can add embellishments, such as underarm turns to steps 1–16.

APPENDICES

WHERE TO DANCE

American Legion/Elks/Knights of Columbus/Moose/VFW

Some of these organizations sponsor their own dances for members only with newcomers admitted as guests of current members. Some rent space to other clubs who sponsor dances which are open to the public.

Chamber of Commerce

Contact your local Chamber of Commerce for lists of organizations that sponsor dance lessons and dances.

College Ballroom Dance Association

Contact President, Edith Gardner, 9129 LaRivera Dr., Sacramento, CA 95826 (916) 362–5094. Information regarding college dance programs and clubs.

Newspapers

Check your local newspaper's community calendar for dances in your area.

Recreation Departments

Some sponsor dances.

Telephone Directory

Check the Yellow Pages under "ballroom" for lists of local ballrooms. Check the "Dancing Instruction" heading for lists of dance studios who offer ballroom lessons; many of these studios sponsor weekly dances which are sometimes open to the public.

Universities, Colleges, and Community Education Programs

Many have ballroom dance clubs that hold dances.

YMCA/YWCA

Some Y's sponsor their own dances and some rent space to ballroom dance clubs.

USABDA

The United States Amateur Ballroom Dancers Association, 1–800–447–9047, can furnish information about places to dance, compete and take instruction throughout the U.S.

Before you go to a new dance, to avoid embarrassment, be sure that you make inquiries regarding attire, type of music, cost of admission, age of participants and whether people come as couples or as singles.

DANCE PROVERBS

Don't start nothing yuh can't finish. Eugene O'Neill

Hand by the head keeps the lady on balance.

He who starts on the downbeat is rarely a deadbeat.

It takes two to tango. Al Hoffman and Dick Manning

Joe Montana you're not; only spread your feet as wide as the shoulders you've got.

Nose follows toes.

Only one can lead.

The faster the music, the smaller the step.

The rule of thumb keeps thumbs at eye level and pressed together.

They also serve who only stand and wait. John Milton

When your balance flies out the door, bring your weight forward to be stable once more.

GLOSSARY

against line of dance A clockwise movement around the dance floor. (pp. 15–16)

alignment Refers to an imaginary line drawn through the center of the body; see (p. 1); see also direction of movement.

and Refers to timing; it marks the half beat of music or the second of three quicks as in "one and two."

backing line of dance Counterclockwise movement with the dancer's back facing line of dance. (pp. 15–16)

ball change A change of weight from the ball of the first foot to the other foot.

basic The step pattern which establishes the normal rhythm and so is considered the foundation for the other steps. Some dances have several basics.

brush One unweighted foot gently passes by the other foot and/or lightly touches the floor as it passes the weighted foot.

change of weight See weight change.

close A change of weight as the feet are brought together.

closed dance position Partners' bodies are separated by a small breathing space; their dance frame provides connecting points through the hands and arms. (p. 2–3)

contrary body movement position This position is reached whenever either foot is placed across the front or the back of the body without the body turning. (p. 4)

conversation See promenade.

direction of movement The direction or position that the feet and body are pointing in relation to the room; sometimes called alignment. (p. 16)

downbeat The first beat of the measure and the heavy beat, usually marked by the bass or low part of the music.

draw Bringing the free foot slowly as if caressing the floor to the supporting foot.

figure See pattern.

follow   The woman's correct response to the man's proper lead.

free leg   The leg on which there is no weight.

gap   Space between the partners, usually refers to an unwanted space, one that creates an unattractive line or a poor body position.

hesitation   A step that is held for one or more counts.

hop   A jump up and a landing on the same foot.

Latin motion   Refers to the hip motion used in merengue, cha-cha, rumba and mambo. The shoulders are held quiet while the body moves between the knees and the ribs.

lead   The man's indication, usually with his body, of where, when and how his partner is to move.

left outside partner   A dance position where the partners' left halves of bodies are overlapping and where the leader is stepping to the leader's right of the partner's feet rather than directly into the partner's feet. (p. 5)

lindy timing   A special timing used in swing where the normal syncopated 6 count basic is interrupted with added even counts resulting in an 8, 10, or 12 count pattern: 1 and 2, 3, 4, 5, 6, 7 and 8, 9, 10.

line   That which defines the shape or contour; refers to essentially the same things that it does in painting or sculpture. In a painting the artist makes lines on the canvas with his paint and brush; in dance the dancers use their bodies to form the lines.

line of dance   The imaginary counter clockwise line around the outside of the dance floor. Dancers following line of dance move like runners around a track. (p. 15)

magic timing   A 6 count timing used in fox trot. (p. 26)

measure   A grouping of musical beats between two bars.

open dance position   Partners' bodies are apart from one another; they are joined by 2 or 4 hands. (pp. 6–7)

outside partner   A dance position where one half of the partners' bodies are overlapping and where a step is taken to the R or L of both of the partner's feet; sometimes called a parallel position.

parallel   See outside partner.

pattern   A complete combination of movements or set of steps lasting approximately 6–32 counts; sometimes called a step, figure or variation. There are hundreds of patterns in each dance.

phrasing   Fitting dance patterns to the rhythm and/or melody of the music.

pivot   A turn done on the ball of one foot. Pivots may be done alone or with a partner and the feet may be held apart, together or one in front of the other.

promenade   A dance position where the partners form a very narrow V; the man forms his longest possible top line from elbow to elbow; sometimes called a conversation position. (p. 4)

quick   A fast step that requires one count or half a count, it equals 1/2 of a slow; refers to timing.

replace   A change of weight which requires no directional movement.

resistance   The pressure exerted by dance partners; they should be like walls for each other neither pushing nor pulling, but solidly there. Their resistance point is very often a communication point, that is, a point where the woman feels her partner's lead or at the least his presence.

rhythm   A regulated pattern of slow and quick beats.

right outside partner   A dance position where the partner's right halves of bodies are overlapping and where the leader is stepping to the left of the partner's feet. (p. 5)

rise and fall   An up and down movement used in some dances.

rock   A change of weight which may be in place or turning but which keeps the same foot positions.

slow   A step that requires two counts or equals two quicks; refers to timing.

spotting   A technique used in turning to prevent dizziness. The dancer picks a real or imaginary "spot" at eye level and this is the only thing he sees while he turns versus the whirl of color that he would see if he didn't "spot."

staccato   That which is abrupt, distinct, crisp, or knife-life. It can refer to movement or music.

step   See pattern.

supporting or standing leg   The leg which holds the body weight.

sway   An inclination of the body to the left or to the right.

sweetheart   See varsouvienne.

syncopation   Modification of the musical or dance rhythm which results in a shifting of the accent so that a normally weak beat is emphasized. An example is triple time swing where 3 steps are taken to two beats of music.

tempo   Speed of the music; expressed as measures per minute or beats per minute.

touch   Without changing weight one foot is brought to the floor or to the supporting foot.

turn out   An outward rotation of the entire leg from the top all the way down.

upbeat   The last beat of a measure.

varsouvienne   A dance position where the partners both face the same direction and hold right hand to right hand and left hand to left hand; also called sweetheart or skaters position. (p. 7)

weight change   A transfer of body weight from one foot to another.

BIBLIOGRAPHY

Buckman, Peter. *Let's Dance*. New York, London: Paddington Press Ltd., 1978.

A fine history of social, ballroom and folk dance from 1200–contemporary dance.

Francois-Brookes, *Ethnic Dances of Black People Around the World*. Deal, New Jersey: Kimbo Educational Records, 1972.

Gives a brief history and steps of some of the Latin dances; presents them in their earliest form as primitive folk dances.

Haylor, Phyllis, Peggy Spencer, and Gwenethe Walshe. *Ballroom Dancing*. New York: David McKay Co., 1983.

Presents the International style of ballroom dance.

Heaton, Alma, and Don Zimmerman. *Close Dancing with Donny and Marie: A Step by Step Guide to Ballroom Dancing*. Utah: Osmond Publishing Co., 1979.

This book uses footprints to describe step patterns.

Hutchinson, Craig R. A Swing Dancer's Manual. 3409 Silver Maple Place, Falls Church, VA. 22042–3545, (703) 698–9811.

Swing in all its many variations is extensively presented by a member of the United States Swing Dance Hall of Fame.

Monte, John, and Bobbie Lawrence. *The Fred Astaire Dance Book*. New York: Simon and Schuster, 1978.

This book also uses footprints. Presents the traditional dances and also deals with salsa, boss nova, slow touch, hustle and merengue. Gives suggested combinations of steps.

136

Moore, Alex. *Ballroom Dancing*. London: Sir Isaac Pitman and Sons, Ltd., 1974.

The first edition of this book was published in 1936. It deals with the International style of dance, but is filled with important technique for all dancers of smooth dance.

Schild, Myrna Martin. *Social Dance*. Dubuque, Iowa: Wm. C. Brown Company, 1985.

Presents all the traditional dances and merengue. Uses footprints and step by step directions. Gives musical selections for each dance and a suggested sequence of steps.

Silvester, Victor. *Modern Ballroom Dancing*. London: Stanley Paul and Company, 1990.

Deals with the International style of ballroom dance; presents a history of the dances.

Stephenson, Richard M., and Joseph Iaccarino. *The Complete Book of Ballroom Dancing*. Garden City, New York: 1980.

Deals with the traditional dances: bossa nova, merengue and hustle. Gives a list of recordings for each dance; includes a fifty-five page history of ballroom dance.

INDEX